THE AMERICAN PRESIDENCY

THE AMERICAN

A Glorious Burden

Lonnie G. Bunch III ✳ Spencer R. Crew ✳ Mark G. Hirsch ✳ Harry R. Rubenstein

Introduction by Richard Norton Smith

KONECKY&KONECKY

PRESIDENCY

✫ ✫ ✫

The presidency has made every man who occupied it,

no matter how small, bigger than he was;

and no matter how big, not big enough for its demands.

Lyndon Baines Johnson

Konecky & Konecky
72 Ayers Point Rd.
Old Saybrook, CT 06475

EXECUTIVE EDITOR: Caroline Newman
DESIGNER: Janice Wheeler
PRODUCTION MANAGER: Martha Sewall
COPY EDITOR: Jack Kirshbaum
EDITORIAL ASSISTANT: Taryn Costanzo
PICTURE EDITORS: Carrie E. Bruns and Laura A. Kreiss

10 digit ISBN:1-56852-709-8

13 digit ISBN: 978-1-56852-709-3

For permission to reproduce illustrations appearing in this
book, please correspond directly with the owners of the
works, as listed in the individual captions. The publisher-
does not retain reproduction rights for these illustrations
individually, or maintain a file of addresses for photo
sources.

CAPTIONS FOR ILLUSTRATIONS PAGES i–ix: *(iii)* Teddy
Roosevelt delivering an address from the rear platform of a
train in 1902. *(v)* William Henry Harrison campaign poster,
1840. *(vi)* Eagle torch ornament carried in 1860 presidential
campaign parades. *(viii)* George Washington inspecting the
unfinished White House with architect James Hoban.
Detail from photolithograph based on a twentieth-century
⊗ painting by N. C. Wyeth.

The editors wish to thank the photography staff in the
Smithsonian's Office of Imaging, Printing, and Photo-
graphic Services. We especially wish to acknowledge the
following staff photographers who created specially com-
missioned photography for this volume: Jane Beck, Harold
Dorwin, Larry Gates, Richard K. Hofmeister, Eric Long,
Terry G. McCrea, Dane A. Penland, Laurie Minor-Penland,
Richard W. Strauss, Hugh Talman, Jeff Tinsley. Douglas
Mudd of the National Numismatic Collection, National
Museum of American History, also contributed photography.

Manufactured in China

DEMOCRATIC WHIG

Harrison & Tyler.

MASS MEETING.

The Whigs of Pittstown will hold a meeting

at ISAAC BULL'S Hotel, Reeds Hollow, on Saturday the 24th instant, at 1 o'clock in the afternoon. Mr. Charles H. Read of the city of Troy and other distinguished gentlemen will be present and address the meeting. All who are opposed to the measures of the present Administration, and in favor of *HARRISON* and a healthy Reform in the General Government, both of this and the adjoining towns are requested to attend.

Nathan Brownell,	John Vanamee,	Jas. T. Vanamee,	Garrardus Deyoe,
Perry Warren Jr.,	Chas. H. Barry,	John P. Ball,	John F. Miller,
Daniel Fish.	Lemuel S. Finch,	Job Andrew,	John B. Reed,
D. E. Williams,	Joseph Snyder,	R. Abbott, Jr.	Peter P. Abbott,
Wm. Harrington,	J G. Devenport,	James Grant,	Dunning Clark,
Christopher Snyder,	David Norton,	Samuel Hitchcock,	Thomas W Hoag,
Leonard Green,	M S V D Cook,	Amos P. Lidden,	John Abbott,
Abram Francisco,	W A Sherman,	S. H. Vandercook,	William Sturges,
Joseph Boynton,	Wm Golden,	P. Silkworth,	S. S. Hide,
Gilbert Carpenter,	Gilbert Eddy,	G. W. Carpenter,	B. I Carpenter,
Ezra Barnes,	James Campbell,	H. Warren, Jr	Libius Lampson,
Stephen Brownell	Thomas Warren	Timothy B Allen,	Abijah K. Downing,

George Snyder, Stephen Cushman, William Clapp, Wm. Chapman, David Carr,

Pittstown October 11, 1840.

The American Presidency has been made possible by the generous support of

KENNETH E. BEHRING

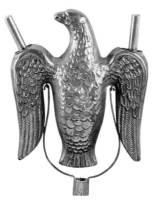

THE HISTORY CHANNEL

✳ ✳ ✳

CHEVY CHASE BANK
CISCO SYSTEMS, INC.
ELIZABETH AND WHITNEY MACMILLAN
HEIDI AND MAX BERRY

Additional support provided by

AUTOMATIC DATA PROCESSING, INC.
KPMG LLP
SEARS, ROEBUCK AND CO.
T. ROWE PRICE ASSOCIATES, INC.

CONTENTS

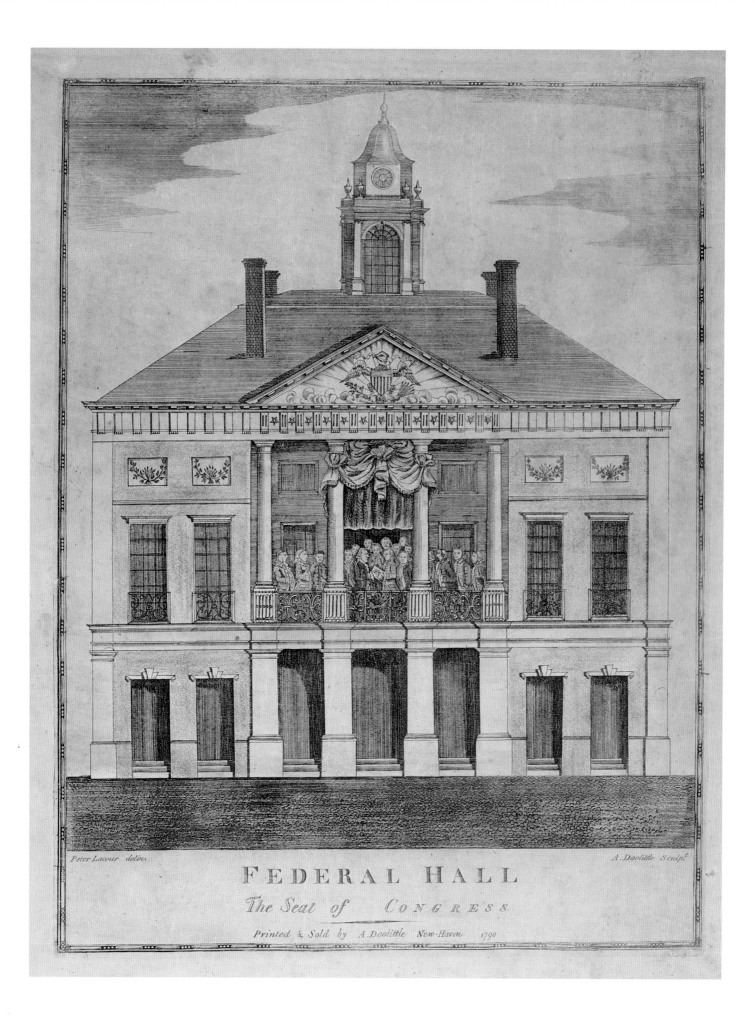

Peter Lacour delin.   A. Doolittle Sculp.

FEDERAL HALL

The Seat of Congress

Printed & Sold by A. Doolittle New-Haven 1790

FOREWORD

George Washington delivered his first presidential inaugural address on Thursday, April 30, 1789, before a joint session of the two houses of Congress assembled within the Senate Chamber of Federal Hall on Wall Street in New York City. The new office he assumed had not as yet been defined in practice by the character and actions of any man, but Washington was wise enough to take the measure of the presidency right from the start. When he expressed a degree of diffidence about being equal to the responsibilities of the office, he might have been speaking as well for all those who would succeed him: "The magnitude and difficulty of the trust to which the voice of my country called me, being sufficient to awaken in the wisest and most experienced of her citizens a distrustful scrutiny into his qualifications, could not but overwhelm with despondence one who (inheriting inferior endowments from nature and unpracticed in the duties of civil administration) ought to be peculiarly conscious of his own deficiencies."

OPPOSITE: On April 30, 1789, Washington stood on the balcony of Federal Hall in New York City and recited the presidential oath of office. This engraving, by Amos Doolittle, is the only known contemporary depiction of Washington's first inauguration. (Courtesy Winterthur Museum)

Washington's modesty was characteristic, though modesty in his case was unnecessary. But he was right to hesitate before the imagined rigors of the office, which makes demands that are plainly unreasonable. How much more apprehensive might he have been had he been able to foresee in detail what the presidency would become over the next two centuries, as the uncertain new nation grew to be the strongest in the world. The Founding Fathers despised the insulated autocracy of a king and created a presidency that flows from the people and is subject to governance by other branches of the government. They would have been amazed, and perhaps dismayed, that the office is now the most powerful political position on earth—far more significant than any of the world's remaining, and largely hollow, kingships.

Many of Washington's successors echoed his sentiments about "the magnitude and difficulty of the trust." Thomas Jefferson, for example, characterized the presidency as "a place of splendid misery." John Quincy Adams could "scarcely conceive a more harassing, wearying, teasing condition of existence" than the presidency. Andrew Jackson called the office "dignified slavery," and Warren Harding complained: "It's Hell! No other word to describe it." Some years before trying it himself, Woodrow Wilson put it this way: "Men of ordinary physique and discretion cannot be President and live."

The American presidency has the brutal power to line a face with age, and to do so more swiftly than ever in an age of instant communications and nuclear arsenals. It is a position for which no training can be adequate, no preparation complete, no counsel sufficient—an office that outstrips anyone's capacity to negotiate the ever-widening circle of its responsibilities. And yet, the presidency is a job individuals avidly seek, a job at which some have even excelled.

Cigar box label.

The American Presidency: A Glorious Burden is the companion volume to a permanent exhibition on the presidency in the Smithsonian Institution's National Museum of American History. The book, like the exhibition, considers the office and the men who have held it from many perspectives—historical, political, cultural, social—but it puts

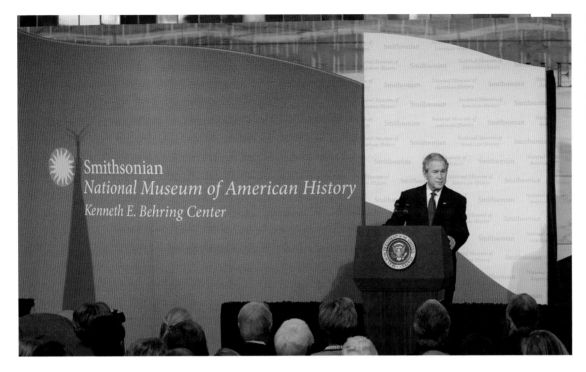

President George W. Bush at the reopening dedication ceremony of the National Museum of American History, November 19, 2008.

an especially welcome emphasis on the human and the personal dimensions. It explores the consequences of asking the impossible of individuals who, no matter what their station in society, are merely ordinary human beings when measured against the majesty of the office. These common citizens persuade the nation to elevate them to uncommon circumstances. There, with imperfect knowledge, they make decisions on which turn the fortunes of the nation and, increasingly, the fortunes of the world.

The circumstances of the presidency may ask human beings to act with greater than human capacities. So they must fall back on their humanity. In the end, character will tell—character that began to be shaped as long ago as childhood, yielding sure instincts, a steady inner moral compass, a capacity for prudent risk, a predisposition to courage and compassion. We can marvel at those whose accomplishments were large and exemplary and sympathize with those who, for various reasons—sometimes, but not always, beyond their control—were not up to the impossible job. Perhaps the successful had intellect on their side (or, more often, *to* their side, in the ranks of attendant advisors), and surely they had luck, but most of all, they had

President John F. Kennedy, January 25, 1961.

character to get them through the urgent moments. The revelation of character through events on a stage as big as the nation, or the globe itself, makes the drama of the presidency, over more than two centuries, incomparably absorbing.

In these pages you will find portrayed both the grandeur of the office of the presidency and the gravity of the personal toll it can exact. Americans ask an astonishing amount of our presidents. We have expected them to be parent, general, diplomat, arbitrator, economist, pitchman, publicist, cheerleader, and a dozen things more—to assume responsibilities from the noble and serious to the barely dignified. We take for granted that the same individual who has the qualities to command armies and deploy an arsenal of awful force will also be available to lead our common celebrations and to shoulder our common griefs, to conclude a school year or launch a baseball season. With all that, we expect our presidents to submit to the gauntlet of immediate and continuous judgment, to the nonstop second-guessing that is the lifeblood of the democratic process.

And our judgments are often summary indeed. To a remarkable degree, every presidency becomes reduced in the popular mind to an association with a handful of events or slogans. We lose the complexity and the nuance in favor of what becomes the iconographic instance: Washington remains the oddly remote "father of his country"; Jefferson is remembered for the (prepresidential) Declaration of Independence and the Louisiana Purchase; Lincoln brings to

In 1776 Thomas Jefferson wrote the Declaration of Independence on this portable lap desk of his own design. Featuring a hinged writing board and a locking drawer for papers, pens, and inkwell, the desk was Jefferson's companion as a Revolutionary patriot, American diplomat, and president of the United States. Among the last documents Jefferson penned on this desk was the note he attached under the desk's writing board in 1825: ". . . Politics as well as Religion has its superstitions. These, gaining strength with time, may, one day, give imaginary value to this relic, for its great association with the birth of the Great Charter of our Independence."

mind an awful war, the Emancipation Proclamation, and the Gettysburg Address; Hoover evokes the Depression; Roosevelt, the New Deal and the Second World War; Johnson, the Great Society and Vietnam; Nixon, China and Watergate. And so on, forward and back. The summary associations are sometimes fair and sometimes not. But they are always too easy, and they favor the slogan over the fine print. This book, and the exhibition from which it derives, will hopefully stir the curious to learn more and to locate the individuals behind the barriers of the slogans.

Washington, D.C., is the home of the presidency and the home of the Smithsonian Institution—America's museum and the repository of millions of items documenting the political, cultural, and social history of the nation. What place more fitting, then, for an exhibition on the presidency than the Smithsonian? The collections of the Smithsonian are filled with objects that reflect the humanity of our presidents, objects that they used and moved among and that furnished their eras. The evidence evokes the men and the office and restores to life the circumstances under which ordinary individuals filled this extraordinary position.

When deciding to mine the riches of the National Museum of American History's collections for items that would portray the nature of the presidency, the authors were determined to show the office as at once incomparably grand and irreducibly human. *The American Presidency* makes clear that our forty-three presidents have been human beings of profoundly divergent qualities and accomplishments. The essays and images in this book return humanity to the office, remind us of its impossible burdens and our impossible expectations, compel us to admire the individuals who, against all odds, met the expectations, and persuade us perhaps to look more kindly on those who fell short.

Lawrence M. Small
SECRETARY (2000-2007)
SMITHSONIAN INSTITUTION

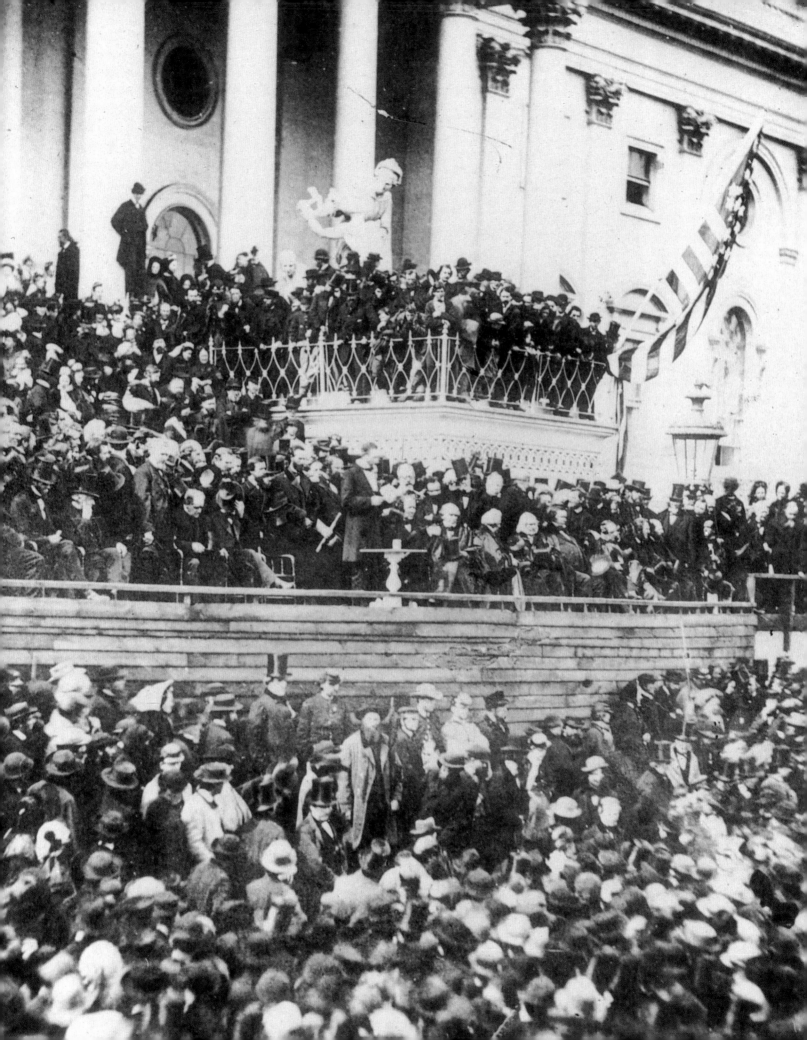

PREFACE

"I do solemnly swear . . ."

With these words, American presidents since George Washington have taken the oath of office. Swearing to preserve, protect, and defend the Constitution and the laws of the land, the president of the United States assumes an enormous responsibility: to safeguard the welfare of the nation as well as the destiny of the world. Few people ever assume a burden so heavy. The presidency, as writer Stefan Lorant noted, is truly a "glorious burden." ❲ This book recounts the evolution of the office of the American presidency, from the age of Washington until today. It examines how the office has changed over time, how the job of the presidency has burgeoned with the growth of the nation, and how the administrations of our presidents have helped to shape—and been shaped by—the American people and the events of their time. ❲ We are especially interested in understanding the culture of the presidency—the beliefs, duties, rituals, and responsibilities of America's chief executive. We are equally compelled and intrigued by the tangible objects, visual representations, and other seemingly

OPPOSITE: Lincoln delivering his inaugural address on the steps of the Capitol, on March 4, 1865, after his election to a second term.

Seated at this table and chairs, Ulysses S. Grant signed the terms of Robert E. Lee's surrender at Appomattox Court House on April 9, 1865. Grant's success as the commanding general of the U.S. troops in the Civil War propelled him into the White House.

In the 1890s, the Republican party sought to attract the votes of working men by promising them "a full dinner pail." This lantern, in the shape of a dinner pail, is from William McKinley's presidential campaign.

ephemeral artifacts that can illuminate little-studied aspects of the presidents' lives and their relationship with the American people. More than wielders of power and influence, presidents through their actions and personalities touch the lives of millions in tangible and intangible ways. They are cultural icons, figureheads of democracy, embodiments of all that is good, for some, and all that is wrong, for others.

Our approach has been to examine the presidency's social, political, and cultural impact on the nation, as well as the nation's impact on the men who held the office. Thus our "take" on inaugurations is that these events are essentially American holidays, moments in which, every four years, Americans can celebrate not just democracy but the fact that our political torch has once again been passed in peace. Likewise, our decision to include chapters on "The Presidency in Popular Imagination," "Communicating the Presidency," "Assassination and Mourning," and "Life after the Presidency" reflects our interest in the cultural and material expressions of the complex relationship between the American people and their chief executive.

The presidency has long been a source of fascination for writers and scholars. Political scientists have studied the contours of presidential power. Historians have written tomes on each president; books on Lincoln alone could fill a library. Journalists have written copiously of their years covering the White House. There are academic monographs on presidents and foreign policy, books on presidential quotes and jokes, compilations of presidential speeches. With literally thousands of books on the presidency, why do we need another one? Why now?

The short answer is that this book was created, in part, to accompany a permanent exhibition on the history of the presidency at the Smithsonian's National Museum of American History. The longer, more complicated answer lies in the opportunity to present and explore the material culture of and about the presidency primarily through the extensive and unique historical resources of the Smithsonian. These holdings tell us much about America's collective memory of the presidency.

Almost from the inception of the Smithsonian Institution in 1846, Americans have seen the importance of saving and donating to the national museum a wide array of objects relating to the presidency. These collections run the gamut from national treasures like the portable desk upon which Jefferson wrote the Declaration of Independence and the stovepipe hat Lincoln wore on the night of his assassination, to more whimsical but no less revealing materials such as the "Teddy Bear" named after Theodore Roosevelt and the pajamas Warren G. Harding wore in the White House. These objects not only speak volumes about the lives of the men who have held the office of the presidency. They also provide a touchstone for America's memories of our most important political leaders.

The objects in the Smithsonian's collections have power: they remind us of how we felt about a particular president or how that president's actions shaped our lives. For example, artifacts from the assassination of John F. Kennedy help us to confront our own memories and enable us to convey Kennedy's importance to the millions of Americans born after November 22, 1963. For older Americans, the microphone used by Franklin D. Roosevelt as he delivered his reassuring "fireside chats" conjures memories of the Great Depression, when money and hope were in short supply. And for all Americans, viewing George Washington's officer's uniform enables us to better imagine the "father of our country."

In a moment of reflection Richard Nixon commented, "once you are in the stream of history, you can't get out." We hope this book provides new perspectives on and a different understanding of the history and popular meaning of the office of the presidency, and of the individuals who are forever captured in this stream of history.

This teddy bear, created by the Ideal Toy Company, was based on a 1902 newspaper cartoon by Clifford Berryman. It showed President Theodore Roosevelt, a noted hunter and outdoorsman, refusing to shoot a bear cub. This story helped cement Roosevelt's image as a masculine but compassionate leader.

INTRODUCTION

RICHARD NORTON SMITH

"There is properly no history, only biography."
Ralph Waldo Emerson

The American Presidency exhibition is cause for celebration by anyone who cares about American history. With fresh perspective and impeccable timing, the Smithsonian presents this most human of political institutions in ways even Emerson might appreciate. In our age of virtual reality politics, millions of citizens wonder if their voices are heard or heeded. Can one man or woman make a difference? If it teaches nothing else, history assures us that leaders of character and courage still matter, that individuals can shape events at least as much as they are shaped by them. Picture Washington on the balcony of Federal Hall, Lincoln proclaiming emancipation, Jackson staring down Southern nullifiers, or Lyndon Johnson telling a joint session of Congress at the height of the civil rights revolution, "We shall overcome." ❡ Writing to his friend John Adams in the spring of 1816, Thomas Jefferson

OPPOSITE: President Woodrow Wilson addressing Congress, ca. 1917. (Courtesy Library of Congress)

Jefferson Peace Medal. (Courtesy National Numismatic Collection)

declared, "I prefer the dreams of the future better than the history of the past." On reflection, Jefferson's alternatives are inseparably linked. Certainly we can all dream of a day when history lives for the average American with a force and relevance that make it an essential part of our culture, even our popular culture.

As it happens, interest in America's past has never been greater—witness the success of The History Channel, PBS's *The American Experience,* and virtually anything from the pens of such literary artists as David McCullough, Stephen Ambrose, and Doris Kearns Goodwin. Perhaps they have been too successful, at least for those historical specialists who disregard the idea of history as a great story—sometimes even a morality play. Sadly, in many a classroom, the statisticians have crowded out the storytellers. But of course it wasn't a statistic that wrote the Gettysburg Address, invented the electric light, or refused to move to the back of the bus in Montgomery, Alabama. No quantifiable theory will explain the Watergate scandal, the psychological magic exerted by Franklin D. Roosevelt in the spring of 1933, or the cranky fortitude with which John Adams courted defeat at the polls rather than yield to warmongers in his own party.

It is only human nature to personalize the past, putting a recognizable face on movements and eras that might otherwise be reduced to academic shorthand. Over the years I have observed that most visitors to presidential libraries come seeking a personal encounter with

Left to right: Egyptian President Anwar Sadat, President Jimmy Carter, and Israeli Prime Minister Menachem Begin relaxing at the Camp David peace talks, September 1978. (Courtesy Jimmy Carter Library)

the president or first lady. They hope to live vicariously for an hour or two in the shoes of a commander-in-chief, to attend a state dinner, to spend a weekend at Camp David, to address a campaign rally, or to ride on Air Force One. The fact that Gerald Ford, born Leslie King, was the product of a broken home, never meeting his birth father until he was 17, may strike a more responsive chord among today's young people than his role in the Helsinki Accords or SALT II.

Office building, museum, cultural stage, campaign headquarters, journalistic nerve center, and occasional war room, the White House is, first and always, a home. Exactly two hundred years after the first occupants moved in, its stately rooms are crowded with ghosts: Abigail Adams lamenting her forced relocation to "the chilly Castle," pacing unheated rooms as barren as her husband's political prospects; the queenly Julia Tyler directing the Marine Band to play "Hail to the Chief" for the president's ceremonial arrival, while she greets guests standing on a raised platform in the East Room dressed in the latest fashion and with plumes in her hair; Mr. and Mrs. Ulysses Grant presiding over twenty-nine-course state dinners and an interior decorating scheme ridiculed as Steamboat Gothic; and a solicitous William McKinley draping the face of his epileptic wife, Ida, in a napkin at the first sign of a seizure, even as dinner conversation swirled uninterrupted around the presidential couple. McKinley's assassination in

September 1901 is but one of the human tragedies that have clouded presidential history. The deaths of eight presidents, the crippling illnesses suffered by other White House occupants, the tension of wartime, the grim tidings of economic distress—inevitably these have influenced and occasionally redefined the nation's highest office.

CREATING THE PRESIDENCY

Long before he displayed in the White House his own stubborn adherence to principle, Woodrow Wilson was a political scientist whose imaginative gifts made him a lively popular historian. In his essay "Mere Literature," Wilson dove under life's surface to get at its teeming, exuberant variety.

> In narrating history you are speaking of what was done by men. I must know what, if anything, they revered; I must hear their sneers and gibes; must learn in what accents they spoke love within the family circle; with what grace they obeyed their superiors in station; how they conceived it possible to live, and wise to die; how they esteemed property, and what they deemed privilege; when they kept holiday and why; when they were prone to resist oppression, and wherefore; I must see things with their eyes, before I can comprehend their law books.

Among Professor Wilson's lesser literary works was a sugary biography of his fellow Virginian George Washington. In more recent years Washington's popular image has transmuted from paragon to prig to slaveholder and expense account abuser. Each February he reappears out of the historical mists, to sell us used cars and appliances before resuming his pose of marbled veneration in a thousand city parks.

Such is the lot of heroes in an ironic age. The Washington that greets exhibition visitors, however, is not the wintry figure embalmed in Gilbert Stuart's all too official portraits, much less the bloodless Saint George stamped on our currency and car sales. Rather, he is a shrewd, charismatic giant who preferred farming to politics, and lost money on both; a reluctant deity who took umbrage at long-winded preachers, deadbeat tenants, and newspaper editors guilty, in his words, of stuffing their journals full of "scurrility and nonsensical declamation" (thereby delivering a complaint echoed by virtually every president since).

President-elect Woodrow Wilson in Staunton, Virginia, 1912.

Washington Peace Medal. (Courtesy National Numismatic Collection)

"I have no lust for power," Washington insisted. This did not mean he had no taste for politics. Indeed, no small part of Washington's political genius was to convince nearly everyone—beginning with himself—that he was no politician. Jefferson may have been more eloquent; Hamilton more audacious; Franklin wittier; Madison more learned; Adams—well, more Adams—yet none of the founders was so shrewd a student of his fellows. "It is to be regretted that democratical states must always feel before they can see," he lamented in the wake of Daniel Shays's pitchfork rebellion in western Massachusetts. "It is that that makes their governments slow, but the people will be right at last." The people, yes, he seemed to be saying, based upon long and close observation of human nature, but hardly "Vox populi, vox Dei."

That our first president might be a man of unsuspected depths, as fatalistic as he was ambitious, would surprise generations raised on mythology and sometimes savage debunking. It was a very human demigod who reluctantly consented to join fifty-four other delegates summoned to Philadelphia in the summer of 1787. Their ostensible motive was to consider improvements to the existing Articles of Confederation, under which a patchwork puzzle of squabbling former colonies had done little to refute Old World skepticism about the infant republic and its prospects. Washington arrived fully aware of his symbolic importance to a nation that was more conceptual than real. His mere presence at the Pennsylvania State House elevated a gathering whose product might otherwise have gone out to the world a political orphan. Delegates never forgot that their own presiding officer, having already exercised administrative, diplomatic, and political sovereignty throughout eight years of war, would almost certainly fill the as-yet-undefined role of executive—if he could be persuaded to risk a jealously guarded reputation.

Henry Knox didn't exaggerate when he said that it was Washington's character and not the freshly signed Constitution that bonded the young republic. At the age of 57, by contemporary standards Washington was an elderly man, convinced that he was living on borrowed time. His hearing was deficient, his memory unreliable. Washington was forced to borrow money in order to attend his first inauguration, a deprivation common to early chief executives. To a friend the president-elect confided that he felt like a condemned prisoner on his way to the gallows. It may be hard to imagine in this era of trillion dollar budgets, but the first president employed more people at Mount Vernon than he did in the entire executive branch of government. The initial federal budget was about $2 million. The United States Army numbered six hundred men. At the State Department, Secretary Jefferson found a toy bureaucracy of five clerks, spending $8,000 a year to administer the Foreign Service, oversee territorial affairs, prepare the census, instruct federal marshals and attorneys of their duties, recommend executive pardons, and correspond with state officials as the government's designated intermediary.

More popular than the federal system over which he presided, Washington showed himself to be a cautious executive, with much to be cautious about. Taking literally his constitutional obligation to seek the advice and consent of the Senate, on August 22, 1789, Washington personally delivered a proposed treaty with southern Indian tribes for legislative approval. Then as now, lawmakers were jealous of their prerogatives. Realizing that no immediate decision would be forthcoming, Washington briefly lost his temper (his secretary Tobias Lear claimed that no sound on earth compared with that of his employer swearing a blue streak). Quickly regaining his composure, the president gracefully yielded to legislative wishes. In private, however, Washington nursed his grievance against the dilatory senators, insisting that he would be "damned" rather than face such public humiliation a second time. He proved a man of his word, with profound consequences for every president since. (The Senate later handed Washington another rebuke by rejecting the nomination of South Carolina's John Rutledge to be chief justice of the Supreme Court, allegedly on the grounds of insanity. In fact the only evidence of Rutledge's insanity was his disagreement with a majority of the U.S. Senate.)

With every action he took, Rutledge's sponsor defined the presidency for his successors. The Constitution, for example, says nothing about a cabinet. It was left to Washington, on his own initiative, to establish one as a sort of privy council. Inevitably, it became an arena of conflict, its protagonists stock figures—or stick figures—in later historical accounts: pitting Jefferson, the worldly aristocrat who lived on a mountaintop and considered himself a friend to man, versus Hamilton, the self-made elitist with a Calvinist belief in original sin, and no shortage of personal experience to vindicate his faith.

Washington Reviewing the Western Army at Fort Cumberland, Md. Detail from a painting attributed to Frederick Kemmelmeyer, after 1794. (Courtesy Winterthur Museum)

(Taking note of Hamilton's reputation during the war, Martha Washington had given his name to the house pet, a large-headed, extremely amorous tomcat.) Each man came to personify discordant strains of political and economic thought. Jefferson the agrarian never got over his suspicion of centralized government or financial elites. Hamilton the mercantile prophet welcomed government intervention as much as he distrusted unbridled democracy. Two centuries later it is fashionable to patronize Washington as an Eisenhower-like chairman of the board, uneasily presiding over an opinionated squad of advisors whose intellectual firepower matched their talent for recrimination. The polite term for this is what constitutional expert Glenn A. Phelps calls "the consultative presidency."

More precisely, Washington the political general had not lost his touch. By keeping each of his talented subordinates inside the administration long after they wished to depart, the shrewd old soldier managed to delay the formal start of party warfare. Indeed, his entire presidency can be seen as an exercise in buying time. In other respects Washington eludes the mold of executive greatness as defined by modern historians. He was no Rooseveltian swashbuckler, wielding the personal pronoun like a deadly weapon or placing his stamp upon the age. He did not become a martyr for a great cause, like Lincoln, or thrill the multitudes with Wilsonian eloquence; indeed, by all contemporary evidence, Washington was painfully awkward when delivering a speech.

In the end, however, the first president proved to be more visionary than his combative advisers. His extensive travels, as carefully choreographed as any modern White House road show, emphasized symbolism (the majestic leader astride his wartime mount Prescott) and meticulous organization (no impromptu speechifying and a thoroughly ecumenical approach to religious and other observances). Unique among the presidential fraternity, Washington was called on to exercise his constitutional duties as commander-in-chief. In the autumn of 1794 he donned his former uniform and led a 12,000-man army into the hills of western Pennsylvania to crush the antitax Whiskey Rebellion. It was Washington who designated a site for the new nation's permanent capital, while spurning the suggestion of a South Carolina congressman that the federal city be named Washingtonopolis. By denying the House of Representatives sensitive diplomatic correspondence relating to John Jay's peace negotiations with Britain, Washington established the doctrine of executive privilege that later administrations would use and sometimes abuse, as during Richard Nixon's years in the White House.

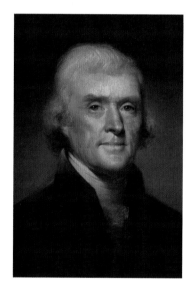

Portrait of Thomas Jefferson by Rembrandt Peale, 1800. (Courtesy White House Historical Association)

No action of Washington's did more to shape the presidency than his voluntary relinquishment of power at the end of two terms—a self-denying measure formally incorporated in the Constitution in 1951. Such renunciation led George III, otherwise no admirer of his erstwhile subject, to call Washington the greatest man on earth. Today he strikes many of his countrymen as being, literally, too good to be true. The poet Robert Frost knew better. "George Washington," wrote Frost, "was one of the few in the whole history of the world who was not carried away by power."

The strong leader of a weak nation, Washington's vision of the presidency was in many ways an extension of his own character. Small wonder that whatever changes are made to the Oval Office by today's occupants, one thing remains constant: a portrait of the only president

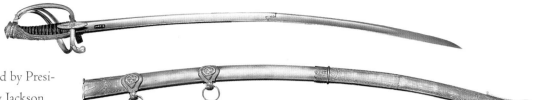

never to inhabit the White House, yet without whose prestige, sacrifice, and political gifts the American republic itself might not exist.

A PEACEFUL REVOLUTION

The opening of "The American Presidency" coincides with the bicentennial of an event second in historical significance only to Washington's 1789 inaugural: the peaceful, if petulant, transfer of power from John Adams's Federalists to the Democratic-Republican opposition led by Thomas Jefferson. An angry Adams boycotted his successor's inaugural, foreshadowing his son's refusal to attend the even more tumultuous inauguration of Andrew Jackson in March 1829. To Jefferson the "Revolution of 1800" was nothing less than the rescue of popular government from aristocratic subverters.

Such views have a melodramatic ring, until one reads the wild predictions made by critics who denounced Jefferson as the infidel of Monticello. Those who regard negative campaigning as a loathsome spin-off of the present age might reflect on what Jefferson's detractors forecast in the event of his election. "Unrestrained by law, or the fear of punishment," shrieked one opposition journal, "neighbors will become enemies of neighbors, brothers of brothers, fathers of their sons, and sons of their fathers. Murder, robbery, rape, adultery and incest will be openly taught and practiced, the air will be rent with the cries of distress, the soil soaked with blood, and the nation black with crimes."

Was Jefferson mentally prepared for such assaults? "No man will ever bring out of the presidency the reputation which carries him into it," he observed ruefully. If he was referring to a reputation for consistency, then Jefferson showed himself to be highly prophetic. No one better illustrates the personal nature of the presidency, or the U-turns of which the political mind is capable. Among the principles for which

Jefferson had staged his "revolution" was a fervent attachment to liberty and a corresponding distrust of presidential aggrandizement. In modern parlance, Jefferson would be the strictest of constructionists.

Yet his nationalist vision overcame his ideological scruples when, in the spring of 1803, Napoleon astonished American emissaries in Paris by offering to sell the United States the entire Louisiana Territory for $15 million in cash. In truth, the West exerted a magnetic pull on this polymath who wrote, "Nature intended me for the tranquil pursuits of science." Offered 828,000 square miles at three cents an acre, and a virtual hammerlock on the rest of the continent, Jefferson readily dismissed his former views about limited government as so many "metaphysical subtleties." And history has been generous to his memory.

AUTHORITY AND POWER

Next to the Renaissance genius of Thomas Jefferson, James Monroe appears a presidential caretaker, a modest man with much to be modest about. Actually, Monroe's personal humility was more than offset by his fierce nationalistic pride. Like Washington, Monroe was more steady than brilliant. This did not prevent Aaron Burr from labeling the fifth president "naturally dull and stupid; extremely illiterate; indecisive to a degree that would be incredible to one who did not know him." It would be fairer to say of Monroe that he was a representative man in an age of giants. Indeed, he has been called "the first ordinary man to reach the presidency." This fact alone did as much to validate the democratic principle as any flight of Jeffersonian eloquence or Madisonian profundity. In 1820 Monroe was reelected with every electoral vote but one, that withheld by a New England elector who insisted on casting his ballot for John Quincy Adams. He did so in part to advertise Adams's claims for the presidential succession, but also to deny the last Virginia president the unanimous acclaim accorded the first.

Portrait of James Monroe by John Vanderlyn, 1816. (Courtesy National Portrait Gallery)

Monroe's consensus was strictly personal. It did not extend to the increasingly vexed debate over slavery in the territories. In accepting the Missouri Compromise, Monroe passively endorsed the first legislative restrictions on human bondage in America. He was far more assertive on the world scene. Backed by that most undiplomatic of diplomats, John Quincy Adams, Monroe's famous doctrine warning European powers against New World meddling derived its legitimacy from a rage for liberty older than the republic from which it issued. But the Monroe Doctrine also represented an important expansion of presidential authority. Although Congress reserved to itself the power to declare war, Monroe and Adams jointly presumed to define the conditions of a just peace.

Portrait of John Adams by John Trumbull, 1793. (Courtesy National Portrait Gallery)

Adams's victory in the disputed election of 1824 introduced even bolder executive claims. In his first message to Congress, George Washington's political heir urged publicly funded internal improvements, roads and canals, scientific expeditions, a naval academy, even a national university and astronomical observatory ("a lighthouse of the sky"). More visionary than achievable, Adams's program would have made the most ardent New Dealer blush.

It is no crime to be ahead of one's time, except politically. As FDR himself once confided, it is a terrible thing for a leader to look over his shoulder and find no one following his lead. Whatever else it requires, the presidency demands political acumen, gyroscopic balance, and a talent for making useful enemies. Therein lies a paradox. Whether it's Andrew Jackson denouncing undemocratic bankers, Teddy Roosevelt savaging "malefactors of wealth," or Harry Truman upholding civilian supremacy by firing General Douglas MacArthur, history's most admired presidents are often contemporary polarizers. They do not hesitate to divide the country, if only because they wish to shatter the prevailing consensus and replace it with one of their own making.

LINCOLN AND THE PERMANENT CAMPAIGN

No one, of course, was so divisive as that ultimate Unionist, Abraham Lincoln. "I claim not to have controlled events, but confess plainly that events have controlled me," Lincoln told an irate Kentuckian who complained that the president had reneged on his pledge not to make war on slavery. What an artful dodge: "Don't blame me—blame events." That Lincoln could shed his skin without losing his soul should hardly

This fence rail was acquired at an 1864 Chicago fair held for the benefit of wounded Civil War soldiers. Its authenticity was confirmed by John Hanks, who maintained that he and Lincoln split it in 1829 or 1830. The prize souvenir of several families, the rail came to the Smithsonian Institution in 1983.

come as a surprise, for this master politician had long since perfected the art of concealment.

In some ways he is hiding still. In the popular mind, Lincoln is forever enshrined as the unlettered genius who came out of the wilderness to vindicate popular government in a world where kings and despots still held sway. The reality is more complicated. In fact, Lincoln spent a lifetime, not so much celebrating his origins as escaping them. It wasn't the $8-a-month flatboatman to whom his political philosophy paid tribute, but a system of government that offered him and other common laborers the chance to be uncommon, to work their way to respectable self-sufficiency and a smattering of culture.

His burning need for recognition was hammered on the forge of adversity. Lincoln's earliest memories revolved around dreary farm labor from which Parson Weems's idealized portrait of George Washington crossing the Delaware had offered an enterprising and imaginative boy momentary respite. Over time the quest for self-control became a integral part of Lincoln's dogged pursuit of the secular immortality bestowed on Washington and the founding generation. Yet some things are beyond control. No amount of virtue or discipline or moral superiority can assure the outcome of an election.

So while there is no single explanation for Lincoln's moody silences or abrupt emotional withdrawals, the most credible of causes may well be the yawning gulf between his aspirations and his expectations. Both idealist and pragmatist, Lincoln the vote seeker had chosen the one profession that guaranteed fame and misery in equal measure. He hungered after more than office. "It isn't a pleasant thing to think that when we die that is the last of us," a youthful Lincoln had remarked to a friend. Had he died in 1849, or even five years later, following his first unsuccessful campaign for the U.S. Senate, the one-term congressman from Illinois would be little noted nor long remembered today.

Whatever else they held in store, events would spare him that fate. The man who took the oath of office before the West Front of the Capitol in March 1861 was scarcely recognizable to his political cronies back home. Standing at last atop the summit of American politics, a divided soul confronting a disintegrating nation, Lincoln had a tran-

Detail of Lincoln from an engraving of his 1862 cabinet by Alexander Haye Ritchie.

Spencer repeating rifle used by Abraham Lincoln for target practice while at the White House.

scendent cause to ennoble his ambitions. Logic told him that it was hypocritical for a nation that professed its love of liberty to keep millions of human beings in chains. Another kind of logic—the compelling logic of the battlefield—would convince him that a war over states rights must ultimately be fought for human rights. Long before his fateful visit to Ford's Theatre, Lincoln's presidency had become a parable of sacrifice, not success as measured by most politicians. Posterity has taken note.

Abraham Lincoln reviewing the Union troops, 1862. (Courtesy Library of Congress)

If war obeys any law, it is the law of unintended consequences. Instead of purifying the nation the fraternal bloodletting brutalized it, coarsening the political atmosphere and setting in motion overpowering waves of economic consolidation. What has come to be known as the military-industrial complex was not, as popularly supposed, an offshoot of the Cold War, but of the Civil War, when double crews worked day and night at the munitions plant of Samuel Colt to satisfy Washington's appetite for armaments, and wartime ingenuity hatched land mines, ironclad ships, telescopic sights, repeating rifles, and minié balls that proved deadly in their accuracy. On his own Lincoln rejected canoe-shaped footwear designed to allow troops to walk on water; rather more diplomatically, the president spurned an offer of elephants from the King of Siam.

Americans before 1860 had little contact with Washington beyond the post office. Commencing with the attack on Fort Sumter, millions looked on in astonishment as distant politicians drafted soldiers for the Union armies, suspended habeas corpus, created a national currency and banking system, redefined the jurisdiction of federal courts and granted vast amounts of publicly owned acreage to homesteaders and land grant colleges. The Internal Revenue Act of 1862 established the first federal income tax in the country's history, a 3 percent levy assessed against annual incomes over $800. The same measure taxed liquor, tobacco, playing cards, carriages, yachts, and billiard tables; it slapped duties on corporate profits and inheritances; and it placed a value-added surcharge on manufactured goods and processed meats.

Fiscal expediencies aside, the war rewrote the nation's organic charter. Eleven of the first twelve amendments to the Constitution limited federal authority. Six of the next seven, beginning with the Thirteenth Amendment that formally abolished slavery in 1865, expanded federal power at the expense of the states. At the same time, generous subsidies fed the extension of railroads and telegraph lines, until the United States in 1880 boasted more rail track than Europe. A government bloated beyond recognition supplied the necessary oxygen to sustain fires of political corruption. Simply put, it had outpaced the office temporarily expanded to accommodate Lincoln's own growth.

THE LOST AMERICANS

To historian Dennis Brogan the Civil War remains "the great purging experience of the American people, their shame and their pride." But what of its aftermath? In popular and scholarly imaginations alike, the postwar years have become synonymous with parvenu wealth, stifling convention, and officially sanctioned thievery. The Gilded Age: the very words evoke airless, cluttered rooms, reeking of macassar oil and genteel hypocrisy. At once ruthless and sentimental, the era stands

Portrait of James Garfield by Ole Peter Hansen Balling, 1881. (Courtesy National Portrait Gallery)

in scandalous reproach to the high and holy work of abolition and the new birth of freedom proclaimed at Gettysburg.

In truth, almost everything about politics in the Gilded Age stands modern convention on its head. It was an age when Republicans were radical and Democrats reactionary, when liberals flirted with laissez faire and conservatives rallied under the nationalist banner. However obtuse they may sound to modern ears, arguments over civil service reform, the tariff, and bimetallism mattered intensely to a generation that followed the flamboyant maneuverings of Halfbreeds and Stalwarts, mugwumps and scalawags, with the same passionate interest it had once accorded the movements of Lee and Grant. In 1896 alone, some five million Americans turned out in person to hear William Jennings

Bryan flail big business and the gold standard—an outpouring of partisan enthusiasm unmatched a century later by Clinton, Dole, and Perot combined.

Grant, Hayes, Garfield, Harrison, McKinley: these are the forgotten presidents, wrote Thomas Wolfe, "whose gravely vacant bewhiskered faces mixed, melted, swam together. Which had the whiskers, which the burnsides; which was which?" They may have worn blue on the battlefield, but in the version of history composed by Wolfe and his political soulmates over the years, they have come to be seen as unrelievedly gray. To most historians the great crime of nineteenth-century presidents is that they don't behave like twentieth-century presidents. Contemporary chief executives dominate their times, dictate to Congress, monopolize the media, and pursue a frenetic activism demanded by a nation of satellite dishes. The first and in many ways the most colorful of the lot, Theodore Roosevelt, set the tone by proclaiming his willingness to lead, though only if his countrymen were in what he called a heroic mood. But heroism wears many faces. A reappraisal of Wolfe's "Lost Americans" is long overdue. No less an authority than Bill Clinton has claimed that Grant, for example, has gotten "a bum rap from traditional historians."

Photograph of Lieutenant General Ulysses S. Grant by Matthew Brady, 1864. (Courtesy Library of Congress)

Meanwhile, present-day politicians have nothing on their Gilded Age counterparts when it comes to a scandalmongering press. In 1884 Grover Cleveland's manful acknowledgment of his illegitimate child earned him denunciation from the *Cincinnati Penny Post* as "A Boon Companion to Buffalo Harlots." Still later, unfounded rumors of wifebeating plagued the Cleveland White House. (So much for the notion of tabloid excesses as a recent development.) Once in office, however, Cleveland showed political courage to match his rugged character. Firmly committed to the gold standard, the president split his own party rather than yield to the free silver nostrums of William Jennings Bryan. Admirers said of Cleveland, "We love him for the enemies he has made," an assertion that might just as well have applied to the

Detail from a photograph of Lucy Webb Hayes, 1879. (Courtesy Rutherford B. Hayes Presidential Center)

White House under Jackson, Wilson, both Roosevelts, Truman, Nixon, Reagan, and Clinton.

Shift your gaze from the West to the East Wing of the White House and a trailblazing first lady deemed by her critics to be overeducated, excessively opinionated, and far too influential in her unelected position. A strong-willed social reformer and deft political operator, she hailed from a long line of fiery crusaders, and for all her attention to the social amenities—whether inaugurating the White House Easter egg roll or launching a short-lived fad with her ornamental haircombs—her real objective was nothing less than to redefine traditional women's roles in America.

Her name was Lucy Webb Hayes. Far from the bluestocking "Lemonade Lucy" of popular legend, Mrs. Rutherford B. Hayes was a feminist heroine, the most popular—and reviled—first lady until Eleanor Roosevelt. "Woman's mind is as strong as man's," she insisted, "equal in all things and his superior in some." When the Civil War broke out and her lawyer husband joined Ohio's Fighting Twenty-Third Regiment, Lucy wished she could raise a battalion of women to serve the Union cause at Fort Sumter. Politics presented another field of action. Despite giving birth to eight children in twenty years, she maintained a lively interest in public affairs. As the wife of Ohio's governor, Lucy visited state prisons and mental hospitals, and she raised funds to construct a facility for war orphans.

In the White House Lucy was an outspoken supporter of female suffrage, a viewpoint to which she converted her husband some forty years in advance of the rest of the country. Outraged that the unfinished Washington Monument should disfigure the capital named for the first president, Mrs. Hayes persuaded the man she called Rud to secure a congressional appropriation and complete the job. The first lady's far-flung campaign for temperance won her millions of fans and more than a few detractors. Lucy soldiered on, crisscrossing the nation, addressing crowds that cheered her ban on alcohol at White House functions.

"Mr. Hayes will, during the absence of Mrs. Hayes, be acting President," sniffed the *Boston Post*. The president begged to differ. Not long before his death in 1893, Hayes, whose reformist sympathies owed much to his tireless wife, remarked to a friend that his marriage to Lucy Webb had been the most interesting fact of his life. It is a sentiment with which many historians would agree. Lucy Hayes remains the gold in the Gilded Age.

ACTING PRESIDENTIAL

Twentieth-century historians lionized "strong" presidents for their willingness to enlist the state in economic planning and pursuit of equal rights under the law. No one more dramatically advanced this view of the modern presidency than the first modern president. From an early age Theodore Roosevelt declared his ambition to belong to what he called the governing class. TR was a godsend to political cartoonists, as entertaining as he was emphatic. A master of the grand gesture, the man dubbed Theodore Rex was not notably self-effacing. Indeed, it was claimed, only half in jest, that in reproducing the president's first message to Congress, the Government Printing Office exhausted its supply of the personal pronoun.

"Rough Rider" Teddy Roosevelt, ca. 1898, during the Spanish-American War.

Politics is theater, and Ronald Reagan was by no means our first actor president. Under the first Roosevelt the White House became a crowded stage, featuring a neverending morality play scripted, directed, and performed by the president himself. His wife said that of all her children Theodore was the youngest, and his daughter Alice shrewdly observed of her father that he wished to be the bride at every wedding and the corpse at every funeral. Whether he was the most effective of American presidents, TR was undeniably the most entertaining. When he died in January 1919, a New York City policeman spoke for an entire nation when he told Roosevelt's sister, "Do you remember the fun of him, Mrs. Robinson? It was not only that he was a great man, but, oh, there was such fun in being led by him."

For Roosevelt himself, part of the fun lay in shaping history's judgment. TR divided presidents into two categories: the Lincoln type and the Buchanan type, leaving no doubt as to which camp he preferred. Modern political scientists use different words to say much the same thing, when they speak of transforming leaders and transactional leaders, active or passive, catalyst or figurehead, bold visionary or defender of the status quo.

Portrait of Calvin Coolidge by Joseph E. Burgess, 1956. (Courtesy National Portrait Gallery)

Of all the distinctions in the English language, the most misleading may well be either/or. This applies with special force to the subtleties of presidential performance. Leaders who espouse timeless principles generally find time on their side. To be sure, life is lived forward, yet history is told backward—that is to say, looking over our shoulder, colored by intervening events and distorted by condescension. Take the case of Calvin Coolidge, in many ways a throwback to the America into which he was born on July 4, 1872.

Coolidge came by his values as the product of rural New England, where democracy and self-reliance were synonymous. Of his Vermont neighbors Coolidge said, "They drew no class distinctions except toward those who assumed superior airs. Those they held in contempt." Consequently, Coolidge maintained a healthy sense of proportion about himself and his seemingly exalted status. As he put it, "It is a great advantage to a President, and a major source of safety to the country, for him to know that he is not a great man." When it came to defining government's proper sphere, Coolidge was a minimalist, not a nihilist. In his first message to Congress in December 1923, he advocated federal antilynching legislation, endorsed a minimum wage for female workers, and urged a constitutional amendment to prohibit child labor.

Belying the later stereotype of a man who measured life with dollar signs, on the 150th anniversary of their independence Coolidge told Americans that theirs was "an age of science and abounding accumulation of material things. These did not create our Declaration. Our Declaration created them. The things of the spirit come first. Unless we cling to that, all material prosperity, overwhelming though it may appear, will turn to a barren scepter in our grasp."

Proponents of the strong presidency take heart from TR's breathtaking assertion of executive stewardship, which justified virtually any act not specifically prohibited by the Constitution. Much less well known is Coolidge's theory of stewardship, employed not on behalf of endangered wildlife or the victims of tainted meat, but the taxpayer. Said Coolidge, "It is because in their hour of timidity the Congress becomes subservient to the importunities of organized minorities that the President comes more and more to stand as the champion of the rights of the whole country."

Unlikely as it now may seem, Coolidge was the most popular political figure between the two Roosevelts. An effective radio star and diligent administrator, he worked longer hours than Woodrow Wilson had before the war, entertained more White House guests than Theodore Roosevelt, and conducted more press conferences each year than FDR. The recently opened papers of White House physician Joel Boone explode the myth of a do-nothing president who slept away his term and reveal just how great a toll the presidency claimed from Coolidge, who never recovered from the 1924 death of his namesake son. "The ways of Providence are often beyond our understanding," a grieving father wrote later. "I do not know why such a price was exacted for occupying the White House." That he blamed himself for the loss of his son helps to explain the emotional depression that shadowed Coolidge's years in office.

It was another depression, following hard on the heels of his departure from Washington in March 1929, which has led historians to portray Coolidge as a master of inaction who, if he didn't actually cause the Great Depression, did nothing to avert it. There is a word for this: hindsight. Presidents can only be understood within the context, conventions, and limitations of their time. Imagine, if possible, an America in which relatively few citizens looked to Washington to solve their problems. If you were Coolidge's age in 1923, during the span of a single tumultuous generation, you would have mourned the assassination of a popular president and watched as his youthful and charismatic successor reinvented the office before splitting the nation's majority party in pique over the performance of his hand-picked replacement.

You also would have seen Woodrow Wilson, the first Democratic president in a generation, take office on a platform of domestic reform, only to be consumed by wartime regimentation, domestic turmoil, and shameful outbreaks of

Detail of photograph of Georges Clemenceau and Woodrow Wilson at the Paris peace talks, May 27, 1919.

racial and ethnic intolerance. The father of the New Freedom would create a host of new federal boards, agencies, and commissions to set prices and allocate scarce resources. The president's son-in-law ran the nation's railroads. Wilson himself was empowered to dictate the price of sugar and the size of baby carriages. If this champion of self-determination overseas remained staunch in his opposition to women's suffrage, he at least liberated American females from the steel corset— yet another military expedient that freed up 8,000 tons of precious metal with which to float a pair of battleships.

In other respects the Wilson years were anything but liberating. Between 1916 and 1920 tax revenues multiplied sixfold. During the same period the national debt ballooned from $1 billion to nearly $26 billion, even as inflation sent the cost of living skyrocketing. Factor in the postwar wave of strikes, redbaiting, and official repression, and it will come as no surprise that voters in 1920 longed for what Warren Harding memorably, if ungrammatically, called normalcy. Unfortunately, Harding's Ohio Gang proved to be a boozy fraternity who looted the public treasury and tarnished what remained of wartime idealism.

Enter Calvin Coolidge, pledged to restore the integrity of his office and destined, more or less by accident, to illustrate one of the alternating currents of presidential history. If America has a civic faith, it is the near universal identification with personal freedom. But what, exactly, is freedom? Each generation defines the term for itself. This helps to explain why leaders come in and out of fashion. History resembles the escalator less than the revolving door. To revert to TR's system of classification, we might segregate presidents into two, admittedly oversimplified, categories: those who would free their countrymen through government, and others who would free them from government. Coolidge was clearly of the second school. As such, it is hardly surprising that he should be held in low regard by New Deal historians. But time has a way of eroding orthodoxy, or at least of admitting doubt.

COMMUNICATING THE PRESIDENCY

Two of the past century's most important presidents personify these diverging schools of thought. "I want to be a preacher president," said Franklin D. Roosevelt in conscious emulation of his colorful cousin. By the 1930s the bully pulpit was electronic: thanks to radio, millions of Americans could listen to a president in their own homes. Shying away from overtly partisan appeals, FDR used homely metaphors to ingratiate himself with listeners around America's kitchen tables. So he spoke of "priming the pump" to justify deficit spending and of loaning embattled Britain a garden hose in the form of Lend-Lease with which to douse the flames started by Hitler and his Nazi arsonists.

A Depression-weary public responded overwhelmingly to the messenger and his message of hope. The actress Lillian Gish said of the new president that "he seemed to have been dipped in phosphorous." In contrast to the single clerk who handled Herbert Hoover's mail, FDR needed fifty to keep abreast of the tide. As the presidency reached new heights of prestige, the rest of the federal government grew in direct proportion to the economic and foreign crises of the period.

Among the countless listeners who drew hope from Roosevelt's honey-on-toast baritone was a shoe salesman's son in Dixon, Illinois. In the Reagan household Franklin D. Roosevelt was an icon and his New Deal programs vehicles of salvation, not least of all for Ron's alcoholic father, Jack, who landed a job with the WPA. Unsurprisingly, young Reagan cast his first presidential ballot for FDR. The Reagan family may have been poor enough that "oatmeal meat" was considered a delicacy, but Nelle Reagan, the Bible-quoting parent who assured Ron that everything in life was part of God's plan, gave him as firm a moral grounding as Sarah Delano imparted to her cosseted only son on his Hudson Valley estate.

Growing up in a household dominated by adults, young Franklin D. Roosevelt learned early to hide his true feelings behind a dutiful façade of smiling aloofness. As president he would have countless acquaintances and almost no intimate friends. Much the same could be said of Reagan, the bookish youth who lived in his dreams and through his mother's fundamentalist faith.

For all their ideological differences Roosevelt and Reagan have much in common. Figures of elusive temperament, each man was easily underestimated.

Franklin D. Roosevelt delivering a "fireside chat."

FDR's automobile lap robe with presidential seal.

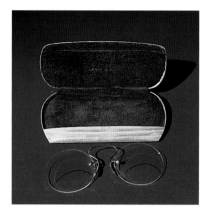

Franklin D. Roosevelt's pince-nez and case.

Each served as governor of the nation's largest state, before entering the White House in a period of grave economic crisis. Each brilliantly used the mass media to enlist public support for his agenda. Each raised the nation's mood through the force of his personality and unquenchable optimism.

During his 1932 campaign Roosevelt declared, "I ask you to judge me by the enemies I have made." In truth both men had a genius for exploiting their opponents—whether the European dictators against whom FDR maneuvered in the 1930s or the Evil Empire that haunted Reagan's vision of a world precariously balanced on the narrow window-ledge of nuclear destruction. On the home front, Roosevelt ran against big business and Reagan railed at the excesses of big government. Each man defeated a predecessor who knew more than he did about the governing process and understood less about the American people. What Justice Holmes said of Herbert Hoover's successor in the crisis atmosphere of 1933 seems equally applicable to Jimmy Carter's, half a century later. Roosevelt, declared the old Brahmin, possessed a second-rate intellect, but a first-class temperament.

Roosevelt presided over the creation of the first atomic bomb; Reagan envisioned a Strategic Defense Initiative, popularly dubbed Star Wars, to end the nuclear nightmare. FDR boldly recognized the Soviet Union in 1933; Reagan shocked the foreign policy establishment in 1982 by consigning the Marxist experiment to the ash heap of history. Roosevelt put the first woman in the cabinet; Reagan named the first woman to the Supreme Court.

President Ronald Reagan at his second inaugural, January 1985.

More modest than the average politician, Reagan said he didn't mind the fawning media coverage accorded Mikhail Gorbachev after the Soviet leader conceded most of Reagan's points to obtain a nuclear arms deal. As Reagan put it, "I don't resent his popularity. Good Lord, I co-starred with Errol Flynn once." His joy in political combat echoed that of his Democratic counterpart. Once, warned by an aide that Republican Wendell Willkie had his eye on the president's chair, FDR removed the omnipresent cigarette holder from his teeth and replied wickedly, "Yes, but look at what I have on it!"

For each man a landslide reelection was followed by a political comeuppance. Roosevelt's too-clever-by-half plan to pack the Supreme Court with justices friendly to the New Deal demonstrated the limits of his normally faultless political judgment. Reagan stumbled just as badly in the Iran-Contra Affair, refusing to acknowledge his error with the same stubborn resolve that made him go through with his controversial visit to a German military cemetery containing the graves of men who had served in Hitler's S.S. In both instances he elevated intransigence to the level of principle.

Not even their greatest admirers would call either leader a slave to consistency. Roosevelt entered office guaranteeing a 25 percent cut in federal expenditures, only to lay the foundation for the modern welfare state. Reagan believed he could cut taxes and grow his way out of the resulting deficit without sacrificing either his cherished military buildup or the social programs that even conservative voters wished to conserve for their children. FDR, the conservative radical, insisted on an economic bill of rights to complement the political rights enshrined in existing law. He forged a new consensus in place of laissez faire, one that accepted as irreversible the growth of the state and the centralization of power in the executive. By contrast, Reagan, the radical conservative, preached the supremacy of market forces, even as victory in the Cold War and the return of power to grassroots Americans resulted in a presidency more visible yet arguably less powerful than at any time in sixty years.

Clearly their similarities are outweighed by substantive differences of outlook and policy. Roosevelt's New Deal was an improvised response to the gravest economic crisis in the country's history. The Reagan Revolution, so called, was firmly grounded in ideological convictions developed over more than thirty years. Nevertheless, Roosevelt and Reagan should put us on guard against applying conventional labels to unconventional leaders. Liberal or conservative, transformer or incrementalist: such terms imperfectly reflect human complexity, growth, and the capacity to entertain seemingly contradictory ideas.

In assessing a president perhaps the only sweeping generalization is that there should be no sweeping generalizations. To be sure, Roosevelt and Reagan both articulated national optimism and the rejection of limits—much as Winston Churchill became the British lion at a critical juncture in his island's history and Charles de Gaulle gave voice to his "certain vision of France" in defiance of the dishonor

of May 1940. Ironically, it is Dwight Eisenhower, their World War II contemporary, who provides the ultimate case study in how presidential reputations can bounce around like corn in a popper.

Never a campus favorite, when he left office in 1961 Eisenhower's standing among presidential scholars was at its nadir. Then, in 1966, the first of Eisenhower's White House papers became available. The next year Murray Kempton published his revisionist essay entitled "The Underestimation of Dwight D. Eisenhower." Before long presidential scholars were competing in praise of what Fred Greenstein labeled Ike's "hidden hand leadership." It wasn't military theater of the kind personified by Eisenhower's old drama coach, Douglas MacArthur, much less the blood-and-guts persona of a Patton. Little that he said was memorable. He conjured no spells like FDR; his speeches were, for the most part, devoid of young John Kennedy's trumpet calls to sacrifice.

So subtle were Eisenhower's methods, so scrambled his syntax, so complete the ruse, that Kempton in describing it had recourse to the nonsense rhymes of Edward Lear:

On the top of the Crumpetty Tree
A Quangle-Wangle sat,
But his face you could not see,
On account of his beaver hat.
For his hat was a hundred and two feet wide,

With ribbons and bibbons on every side,
And bells, and buttons, and loops, and lace,
So that nobody ever could see the face
of the Quangle-Wangle-Quee.

"Innocence," wrote Kempton, "was Eisenhower's beaver hat, and the ribbons grew longer and more numerous until his true lines were almost invisible. It took a very long time indeed to catch the smallest glimpse." Half a century later, scholars are still peeking behind Ike's artfully conceived defenses. Revisionism of a different sort is being made possible by Lyndon Johnson's White House tapes. And as Ronald Reagan's most sensitive correspondence and official documentation is declassified, he, too, will likely challenge the academic consensus.

So put aside the conventional models. The real questions that should be asked of any president are: Did he make a significant difference, not only in his time, but for a long time to come? Did the force of his personality and the power of his ideas affect the way Americans live, how they saw themselves, and how they related to the rest of the world? Did he spend himself in causes larger than himself, for purposes nobler than reelection? Did he take risks for peace, for justice, for national existence?

At the height of the debunking craze of the 1920s, Calvin Coolidge was asked if George Washington's historical standing had been permanently diminished. Coolidge went to the window of his office, pulled back a drapery and pointed in the direction of the nearby Mall. "I see his monument is still there," he remarked. In an era suspicious of heroics, monuments can serve as targets as well as totems. In any case, their fixed, formal completeness bears scant resemblance to an office as unfinished as the nation it serves. Historical assessment is no less dynamic. The presidency reflects the strengths and weaknesses, joys and sorrows, vision and myopia of the forty-two men who have held it. Others may have designed it, but they define it, in the process validating yet another Emersonian dictum: that institutions are but the lengthened shadows of individuals.

President Eisenhower's desk plate.

Suaviter in modo fortiter in re.
Gently in manner, strongly in deed.

CLAUDIO AQUA VIVA

CREATING THE PRESIDENCY

The framers of the Constitution sparked a revolution in government when they created the presidency in 1787. No one at that time, not even the framers themselves, had a clear vision of what the president of a national republic would do. Americans in that age of revolution knew of dukes, burghers, princes, princesses, emperors, lords, governors, magistrates, and monarchs—especially monarchs—but there was no precedent for this new kind of leader. ❡ Americans in the years leading up to the War of Independence came to view executive power as a source of tyranny and corruption. Such power conjured images of King George III. It seemed inconsistent with republican government. So when lawmakers drafted state constitutions in the wake of the Declaration of Independence, they made sure to clip the powers of many state governors. ❡ The social, political, and economic realities of the 1780s prompted Americans to reevaluate their attitudes toward government. The state

OPPOSITE: Late eighteenth-century French engraving of a crowd in New York City pulling down a statue of King George III.

Detail of portrait of George Washington by Rembrandt Peale, 1795.

legislatures' refusal to comply with the laws of Congress, skyrocketing inflation, Congress's own failure to pay interest on the public debt, and the outbreak of Shays's Rebellion—a revolt of discontented and indebted farmers in western Massachusetts in 1786—convinced many Americans that a crisis was afoot, one which could only be brought to heel by strengthening the Articles of Confederation. Expanding the power of government, they reasoned, would not only make America a stronger nation, it would also control what the American Revolution had unleashed: the excessive democratic passions of the people.

The framers of the Constitution hoped to achieve those ends by revising the Articles of Confederation. Instead, they quickly abandoned the articles and invented a whole new plan of government—a "federal" form of government that would be superimposed over the states. And standing at the head of that government would be a president.

Commemorative clothing buttons made for Washington's first inauguration.

The framers cut the presidency from whole cloth. They had no clear model to follow, no blueprint to consult. Questions abounded. Would executive power be invested in one man or in a council? By whom would the president be selected? How long would he serve? What powers would he have, and how would those powers be limited? The framers wrestled throughout the summer with these and other questions. Their answers, contained in Article II of the Constitution, continue to shape the presidency today.

The framers decided on a single executive who would wield extraordinary powers, ones which would far outstrip those of the existing state governors. The president would have command over the armed forces. He would have the authority to direct diplomatic relations and the power to make appointments to the executive and judicial branches. He would have the power to make treaties and inform Congress on the State of the Union. He would recommend measures for the legislature's consideration, receive ambassadors, and ensure that the laws were faithfully executed. He would have a four-year term of office and perpetual eligibility for re-election. And to ensure the president's independence, the framers decided that he would not be elected by the legislature but by "electors" who would cast ballots.

In 1795, toward the end of Washington's presidency, John Trumbull painted these two small oil portraits of George and Martha Washington.

Why did the Founding Fathers, revolutionaries who distrusted centralized authority, entrust such broad, seemingly monarchical powers to one man? The answer lies, in part, in the reputation of George Washington, the hero of the American Revolution. Widely trusted and immensely popular, the father of our country seemed a natural choice for president. But his reputation alone cannot explain why the founders—and, ultimately, most Americans—supported the creation of the presidency. In large measure it was the country's experience after the Revolution that explains why Americans came to accept what seemed unthinkable in 1776: a strong centralized government and a powerful chief executive.

THE NEW REPUBLIC

Now that independence had been won, what would Americans do with it? The Declaration of Independence acted as a guide to the values that the new government should embrace. Having rebelled against a centralized authority, the first inclination was to place most of the power in the states and to limit national authority by establishing a weak central legislature.

However, the realities of building a nation that faced internal disputes and international affairs led many to reconsider the role of the national government and the need for strong executive leadership. Out of this debate emerged the American presidency.

We hold these truths to be self-evident, that all men are created equal, that they are endowed by their Creator with certain unalienable Rights, that among these are Life, Liberty and the pursuit of Happiness. That to secure these Rights, Governments are instituted among Men, deriving their just powers from the consent of the governed. From the Declaration of Independence

2

THE CONTINENTAL CONGRESS

The nation's first governing body was the Continental Congress, established under the 1777 Articles of Confederation, ratified in 1781. It included representatives from each state and was designed to be weak. Bills of any significance needed a two-thirds vote and changes to the articles required unanimous consent. The states maintained a high degree of sovereignty. They coined their own money, raised armies, and erected tariff barriers.

Fearful of centralized authority, the former colonists did not create an independent executive branch. The Congress attempted to handle administrative responsibilities through committees and later through departments with appointed superintendents and governing boards.

3

1 *The Continental Congress Voting for Independence*, engraving by Edward Savage, ca. 1796.
2 French engraving of the First Continental Congress, 1782. (Courtesy Library of Congress)
3 Under the Articles of Confederation, the Continental Congress annually elected a president from among its members. John Hanson of Maryland served as the first such president from 1781 to 1782, but his position as leader of the new independent nation bore no relationship to the presidency established under the Constitution. It was more an honor than a powerful office.
〜 Hanson pitcher, early nineteenth century.

THE CONSTITUTIONAL CONVENTION

Many felt that the Continental Congress was too weak to resolve problems such as the mounting national debt and conflicts between the states. In 1787 the Congress reluctantly called for a convention to revise the Articles of Confederation. Every state except Rhode Island sent delegates to Philadelphia. They were mostly well-to-do members of the states' political establishments. In the end they created a new form of government, with three branches and checks and balances among them.

Only the vaguest notion of the American presidency emerged from the proceedings. Those who followed would have to make this new institution work.

1 The Constitutional Convention met at Independence Hall in Philadelphia from May 25 to September 17, 1787. Fearing that the proceedings would spark public debate, the delegates stationed armed sentinels at the doors and held the sessions in secrecy. ∾ Engraving of Independence Hall, based on a 1778 drawing by Charles Willson Peale. (Courtesy Library of Congress)
2 Engraving of the proceedings of the Constitutional Convention in Philadelphia, by Charles Augustus Goodrich, 1823. (Courtesy Library of Congress)
3 George Washington's general officer's uniform, battle sword, and sheath, 1790s. The ruffled shirt, stock, gloves, and boots are reproductions.
4 This small trunk was used to preserve the papers of the 1787 Constitutional Convention at the Department of State. Convention president George Washington deposited the documents there in 1796.

> [Presidential powers would not] have been so great had not many of the members cast their eyes toward General Washington as President; and shaped their ideas of the Powers to be given to a President, by their opinions of his Virtue.

Constitutional Convention delegate Pierce Butler (South Carolina)

GEORGE WASHINGTON, AN INSPIRATION FOR THE PRESIDENCY

After the war for independence, George Washington was the best-known and most respected of all the revolutionary leaders. Elected to preside over the Constitutional Convention, he helped to legitimize the proceeding and encourage the Constitution's acceptance.

There was little doubt among the delegates that the office of the presidency they were creating would be filled first by General Washington. His reputation was beyond reproach and his mere presence during the debates eased the fears of many delegates that a strong executive branch would naturally evolve into a monarchy.

3

4

In our progress towards political happiness
my station is new; and if I may use the
expression, I walk on untrodden ground.

George Washington

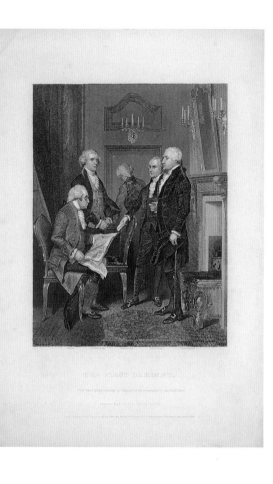

ESTABLISHING THE PRESIDENCY

Participants in the new government knew they were establishing
models for the future. No one was more conscious of this responsibility than the first president.

Always aware of symbolism, George Washington struck a careful
balance between acting too regal and acting too egalitarian. He
chose to be addressed simply as "Mr. President," yet bowed to
guests rather than extending a handshake.

Most important, Washington established the presidency as the
central power of the executive branch. He carefully maintained the
dominance of the office, never ceding its authority to his cabinet
secretaries, never granting its powers to the other branches of government.

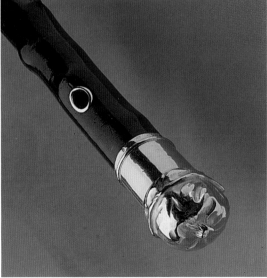

1 The executive branch began modestly with regular conferences between Washington and his four executive secretaries. These meetings evolved into a standing cabinet, a body not specified in the Constitution but, once established, a permanent feature of the executive branch. This engraving of the first cabinet is from a 1789 painting by Alonzo Chappel.

2 Washington lent his considerable reputation to the office of the presidency, thus elevating the position to one of significant prestige and power. In bequeathing his gold-capped crab-tree walking stick, *right*, to Washington, Benjamin Franklin wrote in his will, "To my friend, and the friend of mankind, General Washington. If it were a Sceptre, he has merited it, and would become it." ～ Portrait of George Washington by Rembrandt Peale, 1795.

FURNISHING THE PRESIDENTIAL MANSION

In creating the appropriate personal style for the presidency, Washington modeled its social manners and outward trappings after the southern gentlemanly way of life he had known in Virginia. With no established official residence, Washington outfitted the presidential home in Philadelphia himself with furnishings that were to give the impression of elegance, dignity, and stability. He chose items that were both refined and simple in order to project respect for the office and the egalitarian principles of the Revolution.

2

WASHINGTON'S FAREWELL ADDRESS

The true test of America's young democracy was not the election of its first president, but rather the transfer of the office to its second, John Adams. Near the end of Washington's second term he published his famous farewell address, in which he urged all Americans to support the newly formed nation and put aside regional or party divisions: "Your Union ought to be considered as a main prop of your liberty, the love of the one ought to endear to you the preservation of the other."

1 1830 engraving of Washington's home on High Street, Philadelphia. (Courtesy Library of Congress)

2 Silver-plated bottle stand used by Washington in the presidential mansion.

3 According to family tradition, Washington worked on his farewell address by the light of this brass candelabrum with reflector.

4 This bandanna depicts a laudatory biographical sketch of Washington, with excerpts from his farewell address. It was made by W. Gillespie & Co. near Glasgow, Scotland, late 1790s.

3

4

PRESIDENTIAL CAMPAIGNS

A constant feature of American politics, presidential campaigns have evolved greatly since the election of George Washington. The rise of political parties, the expansion of voting rights, developments in transportation, the proliferation of radio, television, and the Internet, and the recent predominance of political consultants, image-makers, and spin doctors—all this has transformed the look, sound, feel, and substance of this remarkable democratic tradition. ❧ The Founding Fathers knew nothing of the political campaigns we know today. In the early years of the republic most Americans thought political parties were divisive and self-serving, and many, including George Washington, warned against the rising dissension that parties reflected and helped to create. In those years it was even considered undignified for candidates to solicit votes from the people. By the

OPPOSITE: Senator John F. Kennedy and his wife, Jackie, campaigning for the presidency in New York City, 1960. (Courtesy Bettmann/Corbis)

1888 campaign poster.

1820s the emergence of factionalized political parties and the expansion of the franchise required presidential candidates to mobilize popular support for their candidacy. This new style of campaigning, which was based on emphasizing a candidate's personality, achievements, and political beliefs, ushered in an unprecedented era of mass political participation by white males. Presidential campaigns would now resemble rollicking, rip-roaring celebrations, complete with stump speeches, fireworks, and massive street parades. During the campaign of 1840, large buckskin-covered balls bearing slogans and campaign issues were rolled across the country from city to city, spawning the slogan "keep the ball rolling."

The expansion of the franchise also transformed campaigning. The relaxation of property requirements for voting in the early nineteenth century, the suffrage movement in the first two decades of the twentieth century, and the civil rights movement of the 1950s and 1960s greatly enlarged the size and character of the political nation, forcing presidential candidates to appeal for the votes of working people, women, and African Americans.

The campaign trail that we know today was a late nineteenth-century invention. Before then, most presidential hopefuls remained silent or, like Benjamin Harrison, conducted "front porch campaigns" from which they made speeches and greeted visitors. This was not good enough for William Jennings Bryan, who in 1896 inaugurated the first true whistle-stop campaign in American history. Conducting an unprecedented and exhausting campaign, the "Great Commoner" traveled 18,000 miles by rail through twenty-nine states and delivered more than six hundred speeches. The whistle-stop approach would be replicated in 1948 by Harry Truman and in 1964 by Lyndon Johnson, who campaigned aboard the "Lady Bird Special."

Improvements in mass communication further revolutionized presidential campaigns. The invention of the radio and movie newsreels allowed candidates for the first time to reach a mass audience rapidly. The new technology was quickly adopted. For example, the returns of the 1920 presidential contest were read on the first broadcast of station KDKA, America's first licensed commercial radio station. From 1920 to 1950 radio would continue to be the major political information source for most Americans.

The elephant became the unofficial symbol of the Republican Party in the late 1800s. This child's rocker was made for the 1964 presidential campaign.

Along with the donkey, the rooster was a popular symbol of the Democratic Party from the 1800s into the early 1900s. Eventually the donkey won out and became the dominant emblem for the party.
⌒ Mechanical rooster, late nineteenth century.

Television eclipsed radio's dominance during the presidential election of 1952, when an estimated 53 percent of the population watched programs on the campaign. Eight years later more than 101 million Americans tuned in to watch four televised debates between John F. Kennedy and Richard Nixon. Today's candidates rely increasingly on television, spending millions of dollars to communicate their message, image, and personality. During each election year, presidential hopefuls turn to media consultants to package their campaign as well as attack their opponents.

Presidential campaigns today are grueling marathons that take candidates by air from New York to Chicago to San Francisco and back again in a single day. On the campaign trail they typically make speeches, kiss babies, shake hands, pose for photographs, and find other ways to connect with the "average" American. Candidates must raise millions of dollars from the party faithful and corporate leaders, ride buses through the hinterland, and rub shoulders with farmers, factory workers, veterans, and soccer moms. They must sample endless plates of barbecue in Texas, Polish sausage in Chicago, and knishes in Brooklyn, all in an effort to motivate and excite an increasingly passive electorate. They must paint pictures of a better America, make passionate appeals to reason, and stake a claim for moral leadership. Not for the faint of heart, the modern presidential campaign tests the mettle of those who would live in the White House.

In many ways the office of the presidency has become part of a perpetual campaign, in which engaging the public is key to more than an election. Without the support of the public, as gauged by opinion polls and congressional elections, the president is hindered in his desire to lead the nation. That desire continues to attract individuals with imagination, ambition, and a sense of public service. For them the presidency is a great prize—an office of seemingly boundless power from which to set the course of America and the world. And every four years, in a ritual of democracy admired around the world, Americans vote for the candidate who will occupy the highest office in the land.

HOORAY FOR POLITICS

For all the cynicism about politics, Americans have deep pride in the democratic process. During the 1800s Americans transformed presidential elections from the concerns of a limited elite into a massive expression of popular will. From the torchlight parades of the past to today's campaign rallies, participation is the order of the day.

Presidential elections are more than just contests to select officeholders. They are occasions when Americans can engage in a national dialogue. They offer an opportunity to examine the state of the country, and to express concerns on issues often ignored by the news media and political institutions.

CAMPAIGNING

The promotion of candidates among an expanding electorate placed increasing importance on the success of popular political campaigns. With the development of a competitive party system came the development of expendable campaign items in the form of banners, badges, buttons, ribbons, and advertising novelties. Politics drew freely on the evocative imagery of popular culture in promoting candidates and building the momentum of the campaign participation and involvement. These campaign objects represent the confluence of American popular culture and politics and presume a high level of personal involvement.

Before the late 1800s, presidential nominees were expected to stay out of the limelight while their parties campaigned for them. As transportation improved, the popularity of personal appearances and whirlwind train tours grew, and "hitting the campaign trail" became a cliché of American politics. For example, Theodore Roosevelt, William Howard Taft, and Woodrow Wilson all spoke to crowds of voters from the backs of railroad cars during their respective bids for office. Decades later, Harry Truman and Thomas Dewey crisscrossed the country in a nationwide railroad campaign in 1948. Today candidates continue to hit the rails but more for nostalgia and press attention than as a means of directly reaching voters.

∽ General Eisenhower on his campaign train, Evansville, Indiana, September 22, 1952.

∽ *Bottom left to right:* William Howard Taft, Woodrow Wilson, Theodore Roosevelt.

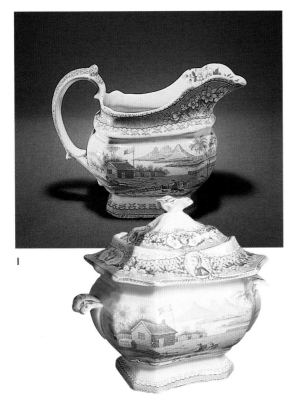

1   2

1 The Whig Party's 1840 log-cabin campaign for William Henry Harrison brought popular electioneering to the masses. Among its many innovations was the sale of goods to loyal backers, such as this pitcher and covered dish with campaign imagery.
2 In the spirit of nonpartisan marketing, manufacturers produce items for all political persuasions. The makers of these cast-iron novelties for the 1908 election created a donkey with the portrait of William Jennings Bryan for Democrats and an

elephant with the likeness of William H. Taft for Republicans.
3 Campaign novelties from the 1964 election.
4 Boxes of macaroni and cheese given as promotional souvenirs at the 1996 Republican and Democratic conventions.

BRINGING THE CAMPAIGN HOME

American campaign novelties are as old as the election process itself. They are created by political parties to promote a candidate and by ambitious manufacturers to take advantage of a market of enthusiastic followers. In an age of television-driven campaigns, such tangible tokens are often dismissed as insignificant. But they help foster long-term party identification and are a way for voters to feel connected to the political process beyond election day.

HATS OFF TO POLITICS

For Americans, elections have always been more than just serious deliberations for choosing a president. Political campaigns are intended to be entertaining and are opportunities for outrageous expressions of

3   4

5 Action figures from the 2008 election.
6 Delegate hat, 1992 Houston Republican convention.
7 Papier-mâché pineapple hat worn by a Bob Dole supporter from the Ohio delegation at the 1996

San Diego Republican convention.
8 "Cheesehead" hat worn by a Wisconsin delegate, 1996 Chicago Democratic convention.

partisanship. Why do political supporters parade around with pineapples on their heads? The only answer is, because it's fun.

TORCHLIGHT PARADES

By the middle of the 1800s spectacular events became the hallmark of American presidential campaigns, and a highlight of every election was the torchlight parade. Hoping to inspire the most apathetic voter to cast a ballot for their candidate, hundreds if not thousands of marchers in cities across the country brightened the night sky in the evenings leading up to an election.

Model log cabin hoisted on a pole and carried in parades by supporters of William Henry Harrison during his 1840 presidential campaign.

Torch, 1860 campaign.

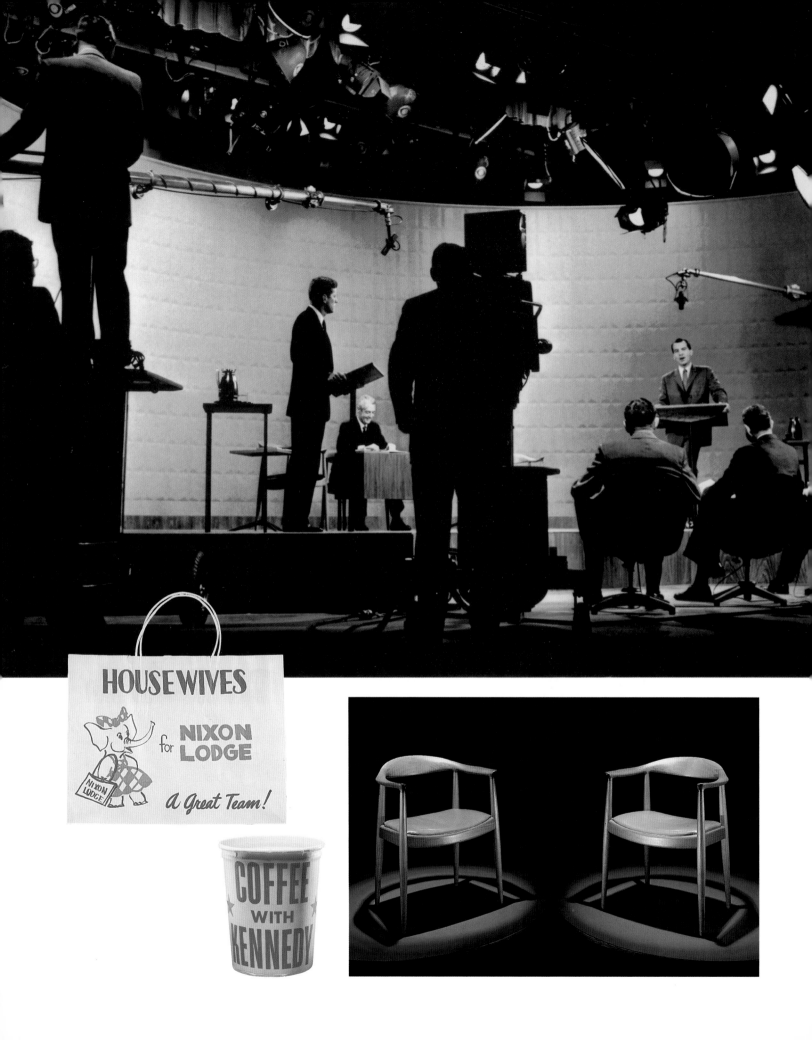

THE MODERN CAMPAIGN BEGINS

In 1960 John F. Kennedy and Richard M. Nixon participated in the first televised debate between presidential candidates. More accurately described as a joint press conference by today's standards, it was a signal event in the history of television and electoral campaigning. The four debates established new standards and expectations for candidate preparation, performance, and appearance.

The 1960 presidential election ushered in a new era of political strategy with the realization of television's power to sway public opinion. Following the debate, CBS president Frank N. Stanton had a commemorative silver plate attached to the back of each chair, identifying its user. ⌁ Kennedy–Nixon debate studio and chairs. **1** In 1987 the Democratic and Republican parties created the Commission on Presidential Debates. This gave the two major parties greater control over these events' process. **2** 1988 League of Women Voters Democratic Debates. *From left:* Bernard Shaw, Senator Al Gore, Jesse Jackson, Governor Michael Dukakis, and Edwin Newman.

The 1996 Presidential Debates

COMMISSION ON PRESIDENTIAL DEBATES

1

2

LEAGUE OF WOMEN VOTERS
PRESIDENTIAL DEBATES

Voting is the first duty
of democracy. Lyndon B. Johnson

THE RIGHT TO VOTE

The Constitution did not specify who had the right to vote, leaving
that decision to the states. At first most states allowed only proper-
tied white males to vote; by the 1820s many property requirements
were dropped. Only after the Civil War did the federal government
enact laws specifying certain national standards.

Slowly suffrage was extended, generally applying today to male
and female citizens eighteen and older. But this did not happen
without the dedicated struggle of those demanding inclusion. Controversy and discrimination characterized the history of voting, as
minorities, women, the poor, and young adults fought to obtain
this basic right of citizenship.

2

1 After decades of protests, women gained the right to vote in national elections in 1920 with the passage of the Nineteenth Amendment to the Constitution.
〜 Women's suffrage protest in front of the White House, February 1917. (Courtesy Library of Congress)

2 The historic Selma to Montgomery, Alabama, voting-rights march of March 1965 drew national attention to the discriminatory practices that barred many African Americans from voting and led to the passage of the Voting Rights Act of 1965.

3 Shoes worn by Juanita T. Williams during the march. (Lent by Rev. and Mrs. Hosea Williams)

4 Banner carried in the voting-rights march.

3

4

ONE MAN
[X]
ONE VOTE

GETTING OUT THE VOTE

Although virtually every group in the United States has demanded the right to vote, many Americans who have this right do not exercise it. In many recent presidential elections only about 50 percent of the voting-age population went to the polls. In the past, local political parties were primarily responsible for getting out the vote. More recently, national special-interest groups have sought to motivate their constituents, who often seem indifferent to the pleas of the candidates.

Political posters, signs, and ephemera designed to motivate Americans to cast their votes come election time.

~ Canvas handbag created to encourage newly enfranchised younger voters to participate in the 1972 election.

No man is good enough to govern another . . . without that other's consent.

Abraham Lincoln, October 16, 1854

The president of the United States is arguably the most powerful and influential individual in the world today. Yet that power is derived from the will of the people as expressed at the ballot box. By voting, Americans have the right, or rather the obligation, to choose who holds this office. And through their vote, American citizens can and do temper and limit the power of the presi-dency. The uniqueness and strength of the presidency comes not from individual accom-plishment or partisan politics, but from the fact that the holder of the office is made accountable by the American public through the vote. Ultimately, presidential power emanates from the consent of the gov-erned.

~ A glass jar ballot "box" used in the Midwest during the 1880s.

CELEBRATING INAUGURATIONS

An array of wonderful contradictions and paradoxes, presidential inaugurals are one of the most American of all our public celebrations. Every four years, amid the pomp and ceremony, the lofty speeches and the crass commercialism, we honor and celebrate the promise of our democratic traditions. ❧ The ceremonies have an air of dignity that is often reserved only for a monarch, yet at the same time reflect our down-to-earth feelings toward politicians. Presidential inaugurals are part celebrations of democracy and part coronations. They are a call for national unity and an occasion for partisan gloating. Inaugurals are populist and elitist, public and private, inclusive and exclusive, commercial and civic. Most of all they reflect the hopes and aspirations we have for the American presidency and our democratic process. ❧ The nation's first presidential inauguration occurred on April 30, 1789, when George Washington took the oath

OPPOSITE: William Henry Harrison delivering his inaugural address on the east steps of the Capitol, March 4, 1841. (Courtesy Brown University Library)

Taft inaugural souvenir plate, 1908.

of office at New York City's Federal Hall in front of a large crowd. The weather was good. Cannons thundered in salute and church bells rang. Garbed in a suit of American cloth, Washington began the tradition of delivering an inaugural address, possibly the first innovation in national politics.

Addresses have varied. At 8,445 words, William Henry Harrison's 1841 speech was the longest in history. He died shortly thereafter. George Washington's second inaugural address (1793) was the shortest: 135 words. But no matter the length, the addresses provide an index into the great issues of American history. They abound with references to America's destiny, westward expansion, the treatment of Native Americans, slavery, the Civil War, taxes, civil service reform, immigration, tariffs, currency policy, monopolies, conservation, Prohibition, unemployment, World War II, the Cold War, civil rights, Communism, and more.

"Ladder of fame" and other inaugural memorabilia.

Some addresses fall hard on modern ears. Despite lynching, disfranchisement, and discrimination against African Americans, William Howard Taft insisted in his 1909 inaugural address that "it was not within the disposition or within the province of the Federal Government to interfere with regulation by Southern States of their domestic affairs." And yet, many of the addresses contain inspiring words for the ages. There is this from Abraham Lincoln's second inaugural address, which trumpeted hope for a reunited America: "With malice toward none, with charity for all . . ." In his 1933 inaugural address, Franklin D. Roosevelt reassured a nation desperate for hope that "the only thing we have to fear is fear itself." And twenty-eight years later, John F. Kennedy declared that the United States would "pay any price, bear any burden, meet any hardship, support any friend, oppose any foe, in order to assure the survival and success of liberty."

The current custom of having inaugural parades on Pennsylvania Avenue following presidential addresses began in 1889. Before then, parades started at the White House and escorted the president to the Capitol. Occasionally presidents simply opened the doors of the White House to the public—sometimes with predictable results. In 1829 a horde of 20,000 inaugural callers forced Andrew Jackson to flee to a nearby hotel while, on the lawn, aides filled wash tubs with or-

ange juice and whiskey to lure the mob out of the White House. Grover Cleveland eventually ended the tradition by holding a presidential review of troops from a grandstand in front of the White House. This procession evolved into the official inaugural parade we know today.

The parades have included everything from a float with a weaving mill (1841), a hot air balloon (1857), Buffalo Bill (1889), John F. Kennedy's World War II patrol boat PT-109 (1961), and a reproduction of Lyndon B. Johnson's Texas ranch (1965). Theodore Roosevelt's 1905 parade was fabulous, including coal miners, complete with headlamps, Native Americans in headdress, the African American troops of the 9th Cavalry, and Roosevelt's own "Rough Riders." Roosevelt's daughter Alice suggested that the president march the vanquished Democrats down Pennsylvania Avenue in chains, but cooler heads prevailed.

The tradition of inaugural balls has waxed and waned over the years. No official balls were held between 1913 and 1929 or during World War II, but they made a comeback after the war. Six balls were held for Richard Nixon's inauguration in 1969, and in 1981, for the first time, a ball was held overseas, honoring Ronald Reagan in Paris.

From the solemnity of the swearing-in ceremony to the slinky, sequined gowns that grace the ballrooms, American presidential inaugurations are testaments to our faith in the permanence of the nation and in our system of government. They are, as George H. W. Bush observed, "democracy's big day."

1

2

3

4

5

A TRULY AMERICAN HOLIDAY

Presidential inaugurations are public holidays, a time when all Americans can celebrate our democratic customs and creed. There is much to celebrate for, once again, America's political torch has been passed in peace.

Heavily symbolic, inaugurations are meant to reflect the transfer of power. The manner in which a new president arrives at the Capitol to take the oath of office and then returns to the White House is decided with great care. Every gesture and decision will be analyzed by the public and the press. Should the party follow traditions or set a new precedent? Should the carriage be fancy or plain? Should the dress be conservative or fashionable? Should the president ride back to the White House in regal splendor or walk as a man of the people? The impression made sets the tone for the next four years in office.

A gorgeous day,
in every sense
of the word.

Harry Truman, January 21, 1949,
inaugural ball

Jubilant Democratic–Republicans celebrated the 1801 inauguration of Thomas Jefferson and the defeat of John Adams and the Federalist Party. This hand-painted banner proclaims: "T. Jefferson President of the United States of America/John Adams is no more."

1 Souvenir Nixon scarf and inaugural programs.
2 Ronald and Nancy Reagan waving at onlookers during his inaugural parade, January 20, 1981.

3 Jimmy and Rosalynn Carter walking down Pennsylvania Avenue during his inaugural parade, January 20, 1977. (Courtesy Jimmy Carter Library)

3

"I do solemnly swear (or affirm) that I will faithfully execute the Office of President of the United States, and will to the best of my ability, preserve, protect and defend the Constitution of the United States."

THE OATH OF OFFICE

Article 2, section 1 of the Constitution requires that before presidents can assume their duties they must take the oath of office. The completion of this thirty-five-word oath ends one president's term and begins the next.

From the day George Washington placed his hand on the Bible and recited the oath, the inaugural ceremonies have been an important symbol of our government's continuity and permanence.

WHY CHANGE THE INAUGURATION DATE?

In eighteenth-century America it seemed reasonable to set aside four months between the election and the inauguration. This would provide enough time to tally the votes, to have the electoral college members send their ballots to Washington, and for the president-elect to organize the new government.

But in the modern world of communications and politics four months was an eternity in which crises could arise or the outgoing administration could do untold amounts of mischief. In 1933 the Twentieth Amendment to the Constitution changed the date of presidential inaugurations from March 4 to January 20.

1 This image of James Buchanan taking the oath of office in 1857 is the oldest known photograph of a presidential inauguration. More than 150,000 people attended his swearing-in ceremony and the parade down Pennsylvania Avenue.

James Monroe began the tradition of taking the oath of office outside the Capitol in 1817, and since then the public has enthusiastically embraced the opportunity to witness the peaceful transfer of power.

2 Suit coat worn by Benjamin Harrison at his 1889 inauguration.

3 Ronald Reagan's second swearing-in ceremony was held indoors because of the severe cold in January 1985.

4 John F. Kennedy invited Robert Frost, then 86, to read a poem at his 1961 inauguration. The presence of the New England poet lent an air of cultural sophistication to the proceedings. However, the sun's glare prevented Frost from reading "Dedication," which he had written for the occasion. Instead, he recited "The Gift Outright" from memory and then sent a handwritten copy to the Smithsonian.

3

4

THE INAUGURAL BALL

Inaugural balls started as single affairs. In recent times they have grown into many distinct festivities. Some balls were selective; others were open to anyone who paid the admission. Some were formal affairs, whereas at James Polk's two-dollar ball for "pure Democrats," a foreign minister's lady reportedly was seen dancing with her gardener. Jimmy Carter thought "ball" sounded too formal and called his celebrations parties. In 1997 Bill Clinton hosted fourteen official balls. Although the number has multiplied, there remains an exclusive atmosphere that proclaims that this is a celebration for the newly instated political elite.

1 Grover Cleveland's 1885 inaugural ball, from *Perley's Reminiscences of Sixty Years in the National Metropolis,* 1886. The affair was held in the then-unfinished Pension Building. (Courtesy Smithsonian Institution Libraries)

2 Scrambling for supper at James Polk's 1845 "pure Democrats" inaugural ball held at the National Theatre, as published in *Perley's Reminiscences of Sixty Years in the National Metropolis,* 1886. (Courtesy Smithsonian Institution Libraries)

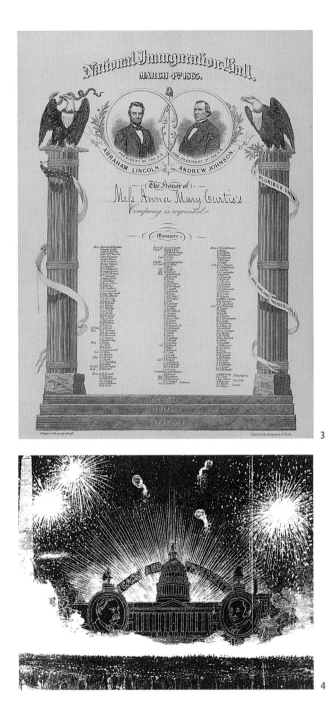

3 Invitation to Lincoln's 1865 inaugural ball.
4 Fireworks display for Grover Cleveland's inauguration, published in *Frank Leslie's Illustrated Newspaper*, March 14, 1885. (Courtesy Library of Congress)

Inaugural ball tickets.

1

2

3

1 George and Barbara Bush at the 1989 Stars and Stripes inaugural ball at the Washington, D.C., Convention Center.
2 Bush 1989 inaugural ball program.
3 Mamie Eisenhower dressed in her favorite color for her husband's first inaugural ball in 1953. Designed by Nettie Rosenstein, the gown is of pink peau de soie with a mauve under-tone, and is embellished with more than 2,000 rhinestones.
4 The Pension Building, now the National Build-ing Museum, sparkled with thousands of elec-tric lights for William McKinley's second inau-gural ball in 1901. (Photograph by Frances Benjamin Johnston; Courtesy Library of Congress)
5 Bill Clinton, *left*, play-ing his saxophone at the 1993 National Building Museum inaugural ball.

PRESIDENTIAL ROLES

As President Warren G. Harding said: "My God, this is a hell of a job!" ❡ As a nation, we place no greater responsibility on any one individual than we do on the president. Could any job be more demanding and complex? We ask the president to be executive, diplomat, and consoler for countless tragedies. On any given day the president might have to make life and death decisions, propose policies that will change the course of the country, and then be expected to greet a group of elementary school children. His tasks are many; his time short. ❡ The president's responsibilities have grown with the nation itself. In Thomas Jefferson's day the entire executive branch consisted of 6,479 military personnel, 1,223 collectors of revenue, 947 deputy postmasters, and 588 others. By the 1990s the federal payroll had mushroomed to 2.5 million employees. To manage a bureaucracy of this size and complexity the nation's chief executive must maintain a huge staff: some 3,400

OPPOSITE: President Richard Nixon and his Secretary of State Henry Kissinger meeting at the White House, February 10, 1971. (Courtesy Fred J. Maroon)

Over time, Americans have increasingly extended more power to the office of the presidency and have expected the individual who holds that office to steer the ship of state safely through uncertain waters. FDR clock, 1930s.

President Theodore Roosevelt convening with a group on the south lawn of the White House, 1909.

people in the 1990s. Personal character has also shaped the contours of the president's job. And when it comes to character, no president has had more than Theodore Roosevelt. With his big grin, buck teeth, pince-nez, and bulbous nose, Roosevelt was endowed with an ebullient public personality that endeared him to the masses. Building on the legacy of Andrew Jackson, James Polk, and Abraham Lincoln, Roosevelt brought to his office a broad conception of its powers, and helped to transform the presidency into what it is today: the center of national political life.

Viewing the presidency as "a bully pulpit" from which to reshape America and the world, Roosevelt extended the government's regulatory authority, pressured Congress to enact consumer legislation, developed aggressive conservation policies, and proposed

Sun watch given to President Harding by the Boy Scouts of America.

an eight-hour day for workers, inheritance and income taxes, and regulation of the stock market. "I believe in a strong executive," he once remarked. "I believe in power."

National events have also transformed the presidency. During the Civil War, Abraham Lincoln stretched the powers of the office further than any previous president when he invoked the commander-in-chief clause of the Constitution to mobilize the Union army, wage war, and emancipate slaves. Likewise, the Great Depression, which left millions of Americans jobless, hopeless, and dispossessed, thrust Franklin D. Roosevelt into the role of presidential innovator. Under his leadership the presidency became a font of social experimentation, spawning dozens of social programs to relieve unemployment and fix America's crippled economic engine.

International events, too, have placed new responsibilities on the president. Foreign relations have always been a focus of presidential concern, but the coming of the Cold War, the specter of nuclear war, international terrorism, the breakup of the Soviet Union, and the emergence of the new world economy have all increasingly led the president to the center of the international arena. For many Americans, the president seems uniquely positioned to ensure the stability of both the nation and the world.

The expansion of presidential power in the twentieth century has promoted great, even impossible, expectations of our presidents. Today we expect him to win wars, resist terror, maintain economic prosperity, save the environment, defend human rights, fight crime and drugs, and show fiscal responsibility. We also want him to symbolize the manners and morals of the nation, a task which is impossible yet irresistible.

Which brings us back to Harding. "My God, this is a hell of a job!"

Paper fan with portraits of President Roosevelt and his 1933 cabinet.

President Eisenhower's reading copy of his 1960 State of the Union Address, containing notes and last-minute changes.

MR. PRESIDENT
MR. SPEAKER
MEMBERS OF THE 86th CONGRESS
FRIENDS

SEVEN YEARS AGO I entered my present office with one long-held resolve over-riding all others.

I was then, and remain now, determined that the United States shall become an ever more potent resource for the cause of peace -- realizing that peace cannot be for ourselves alone, but for peoples everywhere.

Box with gold nugget presented to President Lincoln by the citizens of San Francisco, September 22, 1864.

> Being a president is like riding a tiger. A man has to keep on riding or be swallowed. *Harry S. Truman*

COMMANDER-IN-CHIEF

In times of war and peace the framers of the Constitution wanted to preserve civil authority over the military and so designated the president as "the Commander in Chief of the Army and Navy of the United States." During national crises and war the power of the presidency has increased to include the approval of military tactics, control of the economy, and the authority to limit the civil rights of Americans at home. This power and responsibility has grown dramatically from the days when Washington took up his sword during the Whiskey Rebellion to Truman authorizing the dropping of the atomic bomb on Japan. The burden of this awesome power now rests heavily on every president.

1 In February 1945, the Big Three Allied leaders met at the Yalta [Crimea] Conference to plan the final defeat and occupation of Nazi Germany. *Left to right:* British Prime Minister Winston S. Churchill, President Franklin D. Roosevelt, and Soviet Premier Josef Stalin. (Courtesy National Archives)

2 President Washington, as commander-in-chief, strapped on his Revolutionary War battle sword to review federal troops assembled to put down the Whiskey Rebellion of 1794 in western Pennsylvania. The military might of the president has grown ever since.

~ Hanger-type battle sword and scabbard with silver and green ivory grip made by J. Bailey of New York.

3 While encouraged to leave tactical operations to the military, several presidents have felt the urge to command, and as commander-in-chief they have this right. During the Civil War, Abraham Lincoln, frustrated by the slow advance of General George McClellan's Union forces, personally scouted river landings into Virginia. Lincoln is shown here reviewing the troops on October 3, 1862, in Antietam, Maryland. (Courtesy Library of Congress)

4 Front page of the Washington *Evening Star,* August 8, 1945, describing the damage done from the dropping of the atomic bomb on Hiroshima, Japan, two days earlier. Since President Truman authorized the use of atomic weapons to end World War II, the responsibility of overseeing this destructive force has been placed on every president.

5 Presidents must be prepared to shift agendas at any moment and take on the difficult responsibilities of commander in chief. Here President George W. Bush addressed his National Security Council in the White House cabinet room on September 12, 2001 —the day after terrorists attacked the World Trade Center in New York and the Pentagon building by Washington, D.C. (Courtesy White House)

6 This innocuous briefcase, referred to as "the football," is always carried in the shadow of the president and contains materials that he might need in case of a military emergency.

1

70

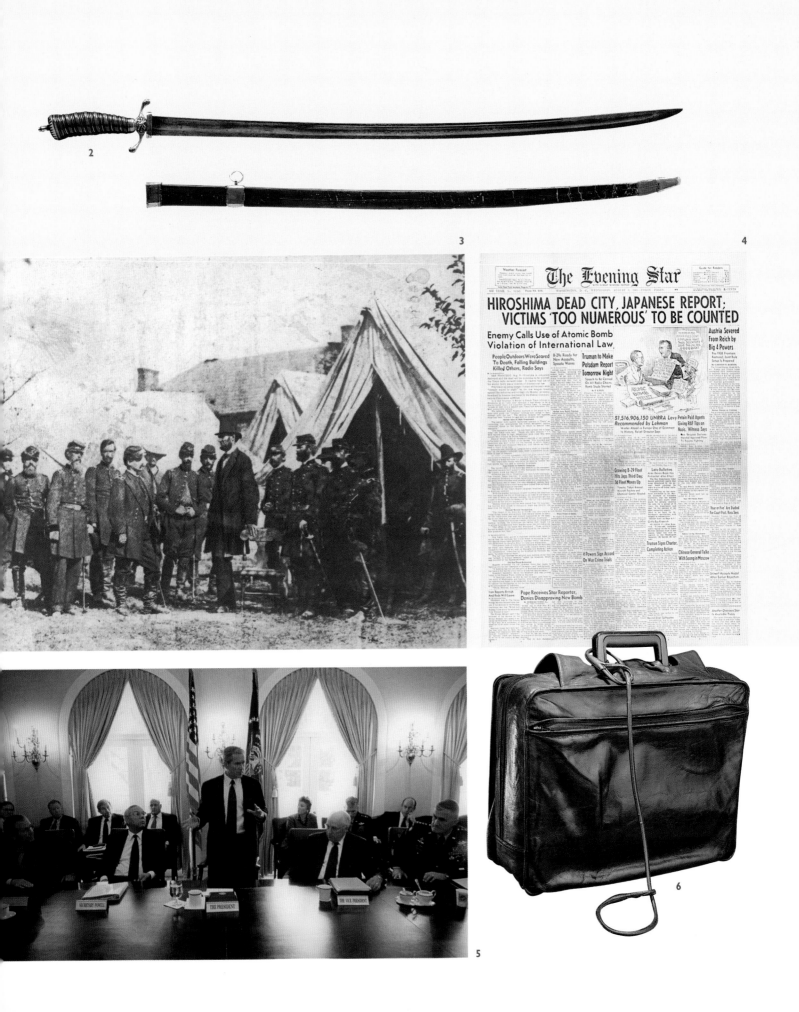

MILITARY HEROES

Beginning with George Washington, Americans have often chosen military leaders for their presidents. Military figures have appealed to voters on many levels. Primarily, they were viewed as national heroes who have had their leadership skills tested under the pressure of battle. Having seen the consequences of war, Americans believed these men would be prepared for future battles and would understand the human cost of entering into future conflicts. Adding to their appeal, as soldiers they seem to be above partisan self-interest. Individuals such as Grant or Eisenhower probably would have been elected no matter which party they chose to affiliate themselves with.

How these presidents have done, compared to others, depends on one's own political views. It is fair to say that the military leaders who accomplished the most as president were those who learned to master the political process, in which persuasion is more effective than commands, even for a hero.

1

1 Andrew Jackson's national fame as the "Hero of New Orleans" in the War of 1812 helped launch his political career. He was the second battlefield leader (after Washington) to become president and his success demonstrated the electoral appeal of military heroes. Color lithograph, ca. 1828.
2 The Whig Party, having seen the political success of Andrew Jackson, chose as their presidential candidate in 1840 General William Henry Harrison, the 68-year-old hero of western Indian battles and a commander during the War of 1812. The Whigs' campaign was devoid of any issues, running Harrison solely on images of him as a humble military hero. Harrison won easily, but he died of pneumonia one month after his inauguration.
 ~ Bandanna from the 1840 campaign depicting Harrison as a war hero and his victories at Tippecanoe and the Thames.
3 Propelled into the presidency on the strength of his military successes during the Civil War, Ulysses S. Grant's lack of political experience allowed his administration to drift and become embroiled in scandal. He later commented, "I never wanted to get out of a place as much as I did to get out of the Presidency."
 ~ Matthew Brady took this photograph of Lieutenant General Grant at City Point, Virginia, during the siege of Petersburg, August 1864. (Courtesy Library of Congress)
4 By the end of World War II, Dwight D. Eisenhower, the Supreme Commander of the Allied Expeditionary Forces, was one of the most popular figures in America. Although not a registered member in any political party, he was sought as a presidential candidate by both. Refusing to enter the race in 1948, he successfully won the Republican nomination and the presidency in 1952, with the nation declaring "I Like Ike."
 ~ Summer uniform worn by General Eisenhower while serving as Supreme Commander of the Allied Expeditionary Forces.

I hate war as only a soldier who has lived it can, only as one who has seen its brutality, its futility, its *stupidity*.   Dwight D. Eisenhower

1 Thomas Jefferson's polygraph, made by Hawkins and Peale, produced duplicate manuscript copies as he wrote. Patented by John Isaac Hawkins in 1803, the pens on a polygraph create simultaneous copies of a writer's manuscript. Jefferson acquired his first polygraph in 1804 and made suggestions for improvements to Charles Willson Peale, the owner of the polygraph's American rights. A prolific letter writer, Jefferson called the polygraph "the finest invention of the present age." (Lent by Franklin Institute)

2 Abraham Lincoln wore this black broadcloth office suit during his presidency. The shirt and tie are reproductions.

CHIEF EXECUTIVE

Presidents serve as the government's administrative officer with responsibilities to see that the laws are faithfully executed and, with the advice and consent of the Senate, to appoint officials. They head an enormous bureaucracy that has become more complex as the federal government has grown in size and increased its functions. Through the cabinet and federal agencies the president has the power to influence, no matter how small, every activity of the national government.

1

2

3

3 John F. Kennedy in the White House Oval Office, October 23, 1962. Photograph by Robert Knudsen. (Courtesy John Fitzgerald Kennedy Library)

4 President Cleveland and his cabinet by L. Keppler, published in *Puck*, 1893.

4

CHIEF DIPLOMAT

To the outside world, the United States president is both a national spokesman and a world leader. As a representative of a nation of immigrants with cultural and economic ties around the globe, the president is not only expected to defend the country's national security and economic interests but also to promote democratic principles and human rights around the world. With greater powers and freedom to determine policy, several presidents who have had their domestic policies frustrated by an uncooperative Congress have turned their attention to foreign affairs.

1 Woodrow Wilson received a hero's welcome when he arrived in France for the Paris Peace Conference in June 1919. Though much of the peace treaty fell far short of Wilson's idealist goals, he was able to gain acceptance for his concept of a League of Nations, in which countries pledged to protect each other. At home, however, isolationism had reasserted itself and Wilson failed to get Congress to ratify the treaty. Wilson's last efforts as president were spent in an unsuccessful attempt to build public and political support for the League. Exhausted from a cross-country tour, he suffered a stroke in September 1919 and never fully recovered. *Left to right:* David Lloyd George, Vittorio Orlando, Georges Clemenceau, and Woodrow Wilson at the Hotel Crillon in Paris, France, May 27, 1919. (Courtesy National Archives)

1

2 Edith Wilson accompanied her husband to the peace-treaty negotiations. In appreciation, the people of Paris gave her this brooch, designed by René Lalique, featuring glass doves perched on diamond-studded gold laurel sprays.

2

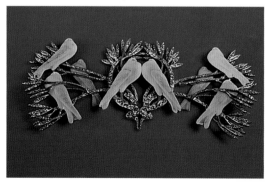

Musket inlaid with coral and silver presented to President Thomas Jefferson by Siddi Suliman Mella, ambassador of the Bay of Tunis, after the end of the Tripolitan War in 1805.

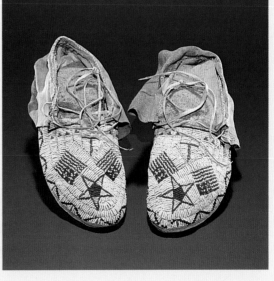

One of the earliest diplomatic issues facing a president was establishing and maintaining formal and legal relationships with the Indian nations within the country's declared borders.

~ Delegation of Potawatomi, Pawnee, Ponca, and Sac and Fox leaders at the White House, 1857. (Courtesy National Archives)

~ Examples of presidential peace medals from the Washington, Van Buren, and Garfield administrations presented to Native American leaders as symbols of diplomatic relations between the U.S. government and Indian nations. The striking of these medals continued until 1889.

~ Moccasins presented to President Grant during an 1870s peace conference in Washington, D.C.

1

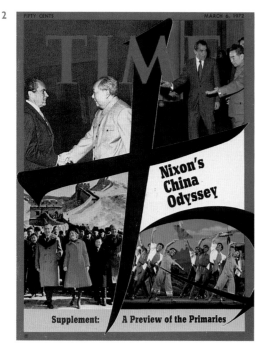

2

1 The use of American presidential influence to settle international disputes has become an increasingly significant responsibility since World War II. In 1978 President Jimmy Carter hosted peace talks between Prime Minister Menachem Begin of Israel and President Anwar Sadat of Egypt. After almost two weeks of negotiations at Camp David, the three leaders signed a peace accord, ending the state of war that had existed since 1948 between Israel and Egypt.

~ *Left to right:* Egyptian President Anwar Sadat, President Jimmy Carter, and Israeli Prime Minister Menachem Begin at the Camp David Accords signing ceremony, September 17, 1978. (Courtesy Jimmy Carter Library)

2 This 1972 *Time* cover captures President Nixon's efforts to ease the strained relations between the superpowers during the Cold War. Through a policy of détente, he became the first president to visit the Soviet Union and in 1972 made his historic visit to China, restoring diplomatic relations after a twenty-five-year break.

3 The increase in U.S. military spending, and the rise of Mikhail Gorbachev as general secretary of the Soviet Union at the beginning of Ronald Reagan's second term, opened a new era of diplomatic relations. Reagan and Gorbachev signed an Intermediate Nuclear Force (INF) Treaty at the Washington Summit December 8, 1987, the first arms control agreement to reduce the nuclear arsenal. The success of these negotiations marked a beginning of the end of the Cold War.

〜 Following the treaty signing, the President and Nancy Reagan held a state dinner honoring Mikhail and Raisa Gorbachev on December 8, 1987. (Courtesy Ronald Reagan Library)

3

DINNER
Honoring
His Excellency
The General Secretary of the Central Committee
of the Communist Party of the Soviet Union
and Mrs. Gorbachev

Columbia River Salmon &
Lobster Medallions en Gelée
Caviar Sauce
Fennel Seed Twists

Loin of Veal with Wild Mushrooms
Champagne Sauce
Tarragon Tomatoes
Corn Turban

Medley of Garden Greens
Brie Cheese with Crushed Walnuts
Vinegar & Avocado Oil Dressing

Tea Sorbet in Honey Ice Cream

JORDAN *Chardonnay* 1984
STAGS' LEAP *Cabernet Sauvignon Lot 2* 1978
IRON HORSE *Brut Summit Cuvée* 1984

THE WHITE HOUSE
Tuesday, December 8, 1987

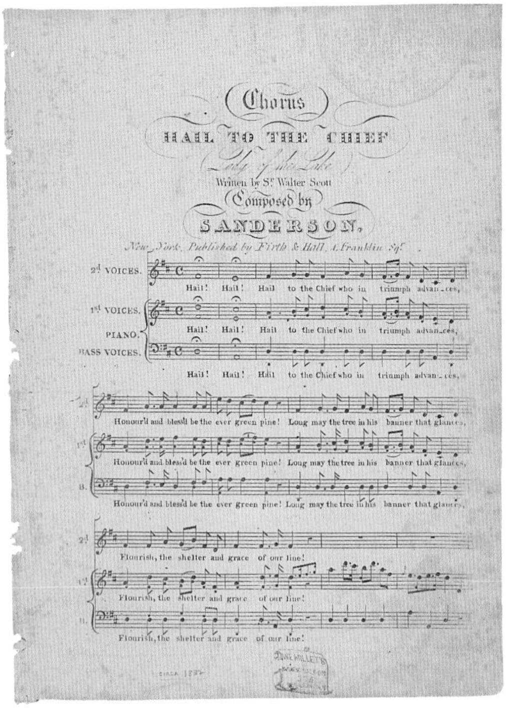

1

2

3

1 President John Tyler's administration (1841–45) established the tradition of playing "Hail to the Chief" as a ceremonial introduction to announce the arrival of the president. The first lady, Julia Tyler, reportedly instructed the United States Marine Band to play the song whenever her husband made an official appearance.

2 The United States Marine Band, established in 1798 and named "the President's Own" by Thomas Jefferson, over the years has provided a regal air to the presidency and the White House.

~ John Philip Sousa directing the United States Marine Band at the White House, May 12, 1930, for President Herbert Hoover, Sir Ronald Lindsay, the British ambassador, and officials of the Gridiron Club. (Courtesy United States Marine Band)

3 Americans expect a certain degree of formality with the presidency but are leery of too much pomp and circumstance. On European visits President Nixon had been impressed by the imperial pageantry of official guards. In an attempt to create a more formal atmosphere for his own state occasions, these uniforms were designed for the White House Secret Service Uniformed Division. They were first worn for a state visit by British Prime Minister Harold Wilson in 1970. The gold-trimmed white tunics and peaked black hats struck many Americans as a comical attempt to emulate the trappings of European royalty. The black hat was the first to go, replaced by a soft white hat. The entire uniform was abandoned during the mid-1970s.

CEREMONIAL HEAD OF STATE

By combining the ceremonial role of a king with the responsibilities of a prime minister, the Constitution elevated and strengthened all the numerous functions of the presidency. Without a monarchy the duties of serving as the ceremonial head of the nation fall on the president. Some of these activities are solemn, such as laying a wreath at the Tomb of the Unknown Soldier; others are more festive, such as opening fairs. These responsibilities can at times seem trivial, but they offer an important opportunity for the chief executive to connect with Americans, who are ultimately an essential source of presidential power.

4

5

6

7

4 Silver and ivory trowel presented to President Ulysses Grant during the ceremonies to lay the cornerstone of the American Museum of Natural History in New York City, June 2, 1870.

5 President Taft throwing out the first baseball at a Washington, D.C., game, June 9, 1902. Taft began the tradition of the president throwing the first ball of the season.

6 President Harry Truman laying a wreath at the Tomb of the Unknown Soldier on November 11, 1947.

(Courtesy Harry S. Truman Library)

7 President Clinton leaving on Marine One, the helicopter reserved for presidential use.

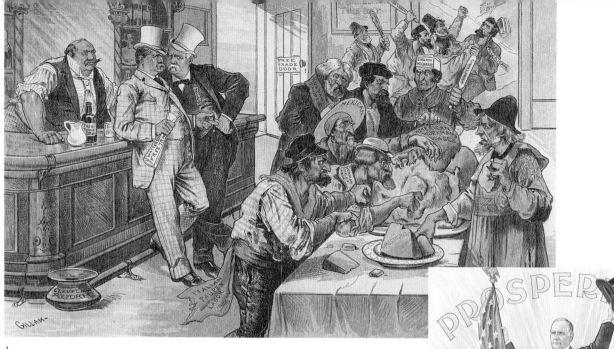

1

2

1 Bartender Grover Cleveland serving up a free (trade) lunch to the workers of the world, *Judge*, 1888.

2 Poster from William McKinley's 1896 presidential campaign.

3 In the name of national security or preserving the general welfare, presidents have used their office to settle labor disputes or affect business practices. In 1894 President Cleveland ordered troops in Chicago to break a strike against the Pullman Palace Car Company that was threatening to disrupt the nationwide rail system. This photograph shows armed federal troops guarding a train during the Pullman strike. (Courtesy Library of Congress)

4 Shantytowns, such as this, sprouted on the outskirts of many American cities in the early 1930s during the Depression, and were dubbed "Hoovervilles" by Americans who blamed the crisis on President Herbert Hoover. (Courtesy University of Washington Library)

5 Wooden bread board from the 1928 presidential campaign, promising continued prosperity if voters elected Hoover.

3

MANAGER OF THE ECONOMY

One of the reasons for calling delegates to Philadelphia in 1787 was to resolve economic problems arising out of the Articles of Confederation. We expect our presidents to keep the country prosperous, to resolve disruptive strikes, keep employment plentiful, and the markets healthy. Even though they have very limited power to control the economy, woe to the president who governs during an economic downturn and is perceived of as not doing enough. The politician in each of them knows what it takes to remain popular. In the words of political consultant James Carville, "It's the economy, stupid."

1

2

PARTY LEADER

The writers of the constitution envisioned that those who occupied the office of the presidency would be above partisan politics. In selecting George Washington they chose an individual who scorned political parties, calling them "potent engines, by which cunning, ambitious, and unprincipled men will be enabled to subvert the power of the people and to usurp for themselves the reins of government." They hoped that those who followed after him would follow his example. They were wrong. The system they created encouraged, if not demanded, a rise of political parties and established that the president either be a leader of the party or an ineffective executive.

For the political parties the presidency is the prize. There are coattails on which to

3

4

1 Banner celebrating Franklin D. Roosevelt's 1932 victory and the end of prohibition.
2 1909 pen-and-ink cartoon by Clifford Berryman showing President Taft handing out "patronage pies."
3 Jackson plate, ca. 1828.
4 Jefferson snuff box, early 1800s.
5 Though many criti- cize the influence of money in politics, presidents are increasingly, and more openly, engaged in fund-raising as part of their role as party leader. At this 2000 gala honoring President Bill Clinton, a record $26.5 million was contributed to the Democratic Party.

ride into office and patronage to dispense "to the boys." Several presidents rose to the office by building political parties or reshaping those that already existed. Thomas Jefferson and James Madison organized the Democratic–Republican Party in the 1790s to counter the Federalist Party of John Adams and Alexander Hamilton. Andrew Jackson created the new Democratic Party in the 1820s and won the presidency in 1828 by consolidating the remnants of the Democratic–Republican Party and attracting newly enfranchised voters. Others such as Franklin D. Roosevelt and Ronald Reagan reshaped their party structures, establishing new coalitions and bringing in new supporters.

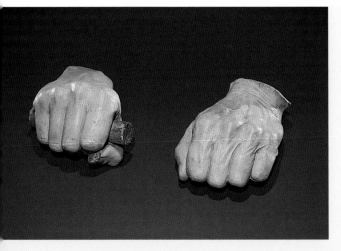

Abraham Lincoln began running for political office at the age of 23 and spent his life as a political activist and strategist. Through Lincoln's skillful political touch he rallied Republican leaders to the cause of preserving the union. These original casts of Abraham Lincoln's hands were taken by Leonard W. Volk on May 20, 1860, two days after the Republican Party nominated the former Illinois congressman as their presidential candidate. Lincoln's right hand was still swollen after shaking hands with so many congratulating supporters.

Volk wanted Lincoln's right hand to be grasping an object. Lincoln went out to his woodshed and cut a piece of a broom handle, which became incorporated in the artist's original cast.

NATIONAL LEADER

Americans ask their presidents to do more than govern; they want them to lead. The role of the president is multifaceted, but no aspect is more important than his responsibilities to articulate the nation's principles, to take on new challenges, to comfort and inspire in times of crisis, and in Abraham Lincoln's words, to appeal to "the better angels of our nature." Although presidential leadership has often been met with contentious political debate, when Americans look back at their history this is the main quality they use when judging a president's tenure in office.

JEFFERSON AND THE LOUISIANA PURCHASE

In 1800 Spain restored to France the Louisiana Territory, creating uncertainty as to the future of America's western border. Through negotiations Jefferson learned that the territory could be acquired, which would resolve potential conflicts with a major European power. However, Jefferson believed in a strict interpretation of the Constitution and was troubled that it contained no authorization for the federal government to acquire land. Jefferson was faced with one of the most difficult questions any president would encounter: When is it right to exceed presidential authority for the good of the country? Jefferson resolved that the chief executive must seize the opportunity and risk the political consequences. He approved the Louisiana Purchase in 1803 for $15 million, thereby doubling the size of the country.

LINCOLN AND THE EMANCIPATION PROCLAMATION

Torn between his desire to preserve the union and his hatred for slavery, Lincoln steered an uncertain course. He feared that if he pushed too aggressively to end slavery he would lose popular support for the Union cause, particularly in the border states. Yet many Republicans in Congress were pushing Lincoln to take a stand for freedom. In the summer of 1862, in his capacity as commander-in-chief, Lincoln drafted the Emancipation Proclamation. For political reasons he waited for a Union military victory to issue the command.

Just five days after the Battle of Antietam, on September 22, 1862, Lincoln ordered that on January 1, 1863, all slaves in states still in rebellion would be "then, henceforward and forever free." The abolition of slavery was now a stated war aim and with Union victory it would be a virtual certainty.

1   Early in 1803, President Jefferson organized an expedition headed by Meriwether Lewis and William Clark to explore the Missouri River and possible routes across the continent to the Pacific Ocean. The Louisiana Purchase in the fall of 1804 made the expedition more critical as it became the first effort to examine the newly acquired lands and to establish official contact with representatives of Indian tribes there.

~ Map of Lewis and Clark's trail, by Bradford and Inskeep, Philadelphia, 1814. (Courtesy Missouri Historical Society)

~ This pocket compass used by William Clark is one of the only surviving scientific instruments known to exist from the expedition, which set out from St. Louis on May 14, 1804. The brass and silver compass set in a mahogany box was made by Thomas Whitney of Philadelphia.

2   A broadside issued at the time of the Emancipation Proclamation.

3   Engraving of the first reading of the Emancipation Proclamation to Lincoln's cabinet, 1862, by Alexander Haye Ritchie from a painting by Francis Bicknell Carpenter.

4   Brass inkwell used by President Lincoln while writing the first draft of the Emancipation Proclamation.

GOD BLESS ABRAHAM LINCOLN FOR HIS PROCLAMATION.

> I want to talk for a few minutes with the people of the United States about banking.

Franklin D. Roosevelt, first "Fireside Chat"

1 President Theodore Roosevelt and naturalist John Muir at Glacier Point, Yosemite Valley, California, 1906. (Stereograph courtesy Library of Congress)

2 On March 12, 1933, Franklin D. Roosevelt addressed the American public over the radio, in the first of about thirty informal "fireside chat" addresses that he would deliver. His ability to communicate over this new medium directly and personally, seem-ingly addressing each listener as a respected friend, gave FDR a powerful tool to shape public opinion.
∼ Columbia Broadcasting System microphone used during FDR's fireside chat radio broadcasts.

3 President Johnson signing the 1964 Civil Rights Act with Martin Luther King, Jr., and others looking on. (Courtesy Lyndon Baines Johnson Library)

2

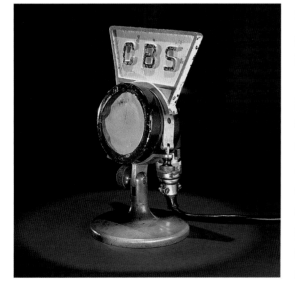

THEODORE ROOSEVELT: THE GREAT CONSERVATIONIST

After the death of his first wife, Alice Lee, in 1884, Theodore Roosevelt sought what he referred to as the "vast silent spaces" of the Dakota Badlands and the recuperative powers of a strenuous life. He purchased a small ranch and reveled in the life of a cowboy. After three years he was ready to resume his political quest in the east.

The experience gave him a love and appreciation for nature that made him a champion of the conservation movement once he became president. Under his leadership the government transferred 125 million acres of public land into the forest reserves, and established sixteen national monuments and fifty-one wildlife refuges.

"The conservation of natural resources is the fundamental problem. Unless we solve that problem it will avail us little to solve all others." (Roosevelt's address to the Deep Waterway Convention, Memphis, October 4, 1907)

FRANKLIN D. ROOSEVELT: AN ICON OF HOPE

On March 4, 1933, Franklin D. Roosevelt became the thirty-second president of the United States. No chief executive, with the exception of Abraham Lincoln, entered the White House confronted by such deep and troubling crises. The nation was mired in its longest and worst economic depression. Approximately a quarter of the work force was unemployed, industrial production was down by a third, and the banking system was collapsing. Internationally the economic crisis contributed to the rise of fascist governments in Europe and eventually World War II.

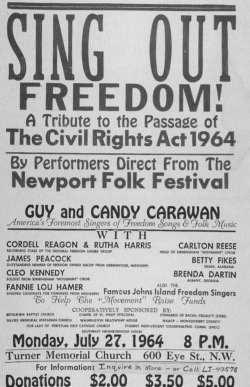

A pragmatist and master politician, FDR boldly experimented with the power of the federal government to address the urgent problems facing the nation. Above all else, Roosevelt's greatest accomplishment was his ability to lead, inspire, and assure Americans through some of the darkest years in the nation's history.

PRESIDENT JOHNSON AND CIVIL RIGHTS

President Johnson became the thirty-sixth president following John F. Kennedy's assassination in 1963. Not willing simply to continue Kennedy's reforms, which were largely stalled in Congress, Johnson declared a war on poverty and an end to racial injustice in America. Using his considerable political skills and arm twisting, Johnson pushed through the Civil Rights Act of 1964, which outlawed discrimination in employment, the Voting Rights Act of 1965, and the Civil Rights Act of 1968 barring discrimination in housing. Together these make up the most significant set of civil rights laws since the Reconstruction legislation following the Civil War.

3

4

LIMITS OF PRESIDENTIAL POWER

Presidents, unlike dukes and dictators, have never been able to exercise unbridled power. Throughout American history their power has been limited by both constitutional and political constraints that have often blocked their programs and initiatives. The Constitution prescribes a system of checks and balances whereby the powers of the federal government are shared among the executive, judicial, and legislative branches. In this delicate balance, however, the influences of the three branches continually shift. The outcome is determined by the individuals in the various offices and their ability to affect public opinion, and by the political, economic, and social climate of the day. ❧ Tension among the executive, judicial, and legislative branches is as old as the federal government itself. After the administration of George Washington, his immediate successors, John Adams and Thomas Jefferson, struggled

OPPOSITE: Detail, engraving of Daniel Webster addressing the Senate, March 7, 1850, by Eliphalet Brown Jr. (Courtesy National Portrait Gallery)

This 1864 anti-Lincoln cartoon, from *Punch*, addresses a complaint of antiwar Democrats during the Civil War: that in order to defend the Constitution and the nation's laws, the President had transgressed on both. (Courtesy The General Library, University of California, Berkeley)

This 1850 print by Nathaniel Currier satirizes President Zachary Taylor's efforts to balance Southern and Northern congressional interests over the question of slavery. (Courtesy Library of Congress)

with political opponents in Congress as they tried to implement their vision of America. The rise of political parties, mass political mobilization, and the increasingly divisive issue of slavery aggravated the political tensions that had existed between Congress and the president. During the sectional crisis of the 1850s, Franklin Pierce and James Buchanan were rendered powerless by an increasingly fractious Congress. The coming of the Civil War saw the power pendulum swing back to the presidency, as Abraham Lincoln, invoking the Constitution, claimed unprecedented—some said dictatorial—authority to run the government. The renaissance of presidential power was short-lived. Following Reconstruction the power of the presidency was generally outmatched by Congress, setting a pattern of congressional dominance that would endure for the rest of the nineteenth century.

Congressional limits on presidential power have recently been joined by a new constraint: divided government. With the exception of just six years, at least one house of Congress between 1968 and today has been held by a party that opposes the president. The result has been an increase in the challenges and difficulties that a president faces in leading the nation.

The Supreme Court has also acted as a counterbalance to presidential power. Even the most dynamic and revered presidents have found their programs contested by the nation's highest court. The New Deal exalted Franklin D. Roosevelt in the hearts and minds of poor and dislocated Americans, but many of FDR's key social reforms were ruled unconstitutional by the Supreme Court.

Public opinion, too, plays a formidable role in limiting presidential power. Often presidents find their vision challenged or changed by segments of the American population who oppose their policies. It was the action of thousands during the civil rights movement of the 1950s and 1960s that forced Presidents Eisenhower, Kennedy, and Johnson to act in support of racial integration and equal rights. Likewise, the antiwar movement undermined President Johnson's foreign policy in Vietnam and played a part in his decision not to seek reelection in 1968. Issues as diverse as suffrage, environmental protection, and international con-

Ticket to Senate impeachment of President Johnson.

John Dean's personal copy of his testimony before the Senate Watergate hearings on June 24, 1974. Dean was counsel to President Nixon.

cerns have also been embraced by a significant number of Americans, whose voice and whose vote have often limited the power and plans of the chief executive. As such, modern presidents have come to appreciate what Abraham Lincoln learned 140 years ago: "With public sentiment nothing can fail; without it nothing can succeed."

Failure to heed public opinion has stymied presidential reelection bids and brought at least one president to ruin. President Nixon's failure to gauge the depth of public revulsion against his administration during the Watergate affair revelations revealed how out of touch a powerful—some have said "imperial"—presidency can be. Having lost the confidence of the people, Nixon resigned from office in 1974.

Impeachment, the Constitution's remedy for removing unprincipled and corrupt presidents from office, is the ultimate check on presidential power. Only two presidents in American history have been impeached. Some Americans fear that the highly publicized impeachment hearings have tarnished the presidency, diminishing it in the eyes of America and the world. But there is also a sense that impeachment has tested the mettle of our Constitution and proved, once again, that our democratic system of government works.

Ultimately, the president's power, vision, and platform are shaped and informed by his ability to work within the limits established in the Constitution and by the voice of the people. That voice, protected by the First Amendment and amplified by a free press, continues to dictate what a president can and cannot do.

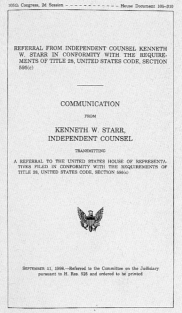

House manager James E. Rogan's trial copy of the report from independent counsel Kenneth Starr's investigation of President Clinton, 1999. (Lent by Congressman James E. Rogan)

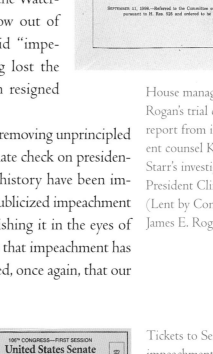

Tickets to Senate impeachment of President Clinton.

In a body where there are more than one hundred talking lawyers, you can make no calculation upon the termination of any debate and frequently, the more trifling the subject, the more animated and protracted the discussion. Franklin Pierce, commenting on Congress

CONGRESS

The delegates to the Constitutional Convention in 1787 envisioned the relationship between the president and Congress as both cooperative and antagonistic. They struggled over how to create the proper balance. Gouverneur Morris from New York, summing up their challenge, stated: "Make him [the president] too weak: the Legislature will usurp his power. Make him too strong: he will usurp on the Legislature." Over the years the balance of power has repeatedly shifted as strong individuals in each branch of government dominated the political arena.

1 Ornate desk and chair sets designed by Thomas U. Walters were used in the chamber of the U.S. House of Representatives from 1857 to 1873. Judge Isaac C. Parker of Missouri used this desk between 1871 and 1873.

2

2 This 1834 print shows Kentucky senator Henry Clay sewing President Andrew Jackson's mouth closed. Jackson's fight to destroy the Bank of the United States and his removal of the Treasury secretary led to the Senate's censure of Jackson for abuse of presidential power. Jackson argued that the president, as the only representative of all the people, should rule supreme. Congress did not agree.

At the heart of the debate (led by Clay, among others) was the struggle between the executive and the legislature over which branch should dominate the government. That struggle continues today, whichever political party is in office. (Courtesy Library of Congress) ∾ Miniature portrait of Senator Henry Clay by J. W. Dodge, 1843. ∾ Straw hat belonging to Senator Henry Clay.

THE SUPREME COURT

The country's final legal authority is the Supreme Court. It has the responsibility to interpret the law and reject legislation or executive actions it deems in violation or in contradiction of the Constitution. Several presidents have seen their powers restricted by court rulings that struck down their programs or restricted their orders.

Since Supreme Court justices are appointed for life, they are largely sheltered from political pressure. All a president can do to alter circumstances is to try to amend the Constitution or hope that vacancies open up on the court, giving him an opportunity to name more sympathetic justices.

1 First photograph taken of the U.S. Supreme Court, by Mathew Brady, 1869. (Courtesy National Archives)

2 Appointed by Ronald Reagan, Sandra Day O'Connor wore this robe on September 25, 1981, when she became the first woman to be sworn in to the U.S. Supreme Court.

3 In the mid-1930s the Supreme Court ruled many of Franklin D. Roosevelt's New Deal reforms, including the National Recovery Act, unconstitutional. Roosevelt countered by proposing to enlarge the size of the court and thus, through his new appointees, win more favorable decisions. Both Republicans and Democrats were outraged by this attack on the court's independence and forced Roosevelt to withdraw his proposal. No president since has directly attempted to undermine the court's constitutional autonomy, and the size of the court has remained fixed (since 1869) at nine justices. ~ U.S. Supreme Court, 1932. (Courtesy U.S. Supreme Court) ~ This cartoon by Elderman appeared in the February 6, 1937, *Washington Post.* (Courtesy *Washington Post*)

1

GROUNDS FOR IMPEACHMENT

The ultimate limit on presidential power is removal from office by Congress through "Impeachment for, and Conviction of, Treason, Bribery, or other high Crimes and Misdemeanors" (U.S. Constitution, Article 2, Section 4). As a political rather than judicial process, impeachment may involve partisan motivations.

Congress has taken its constitutional responsibility cautiously, recognizing that its abuse would end the delicate balance of power between branches of government. Only three presidents have seriously faced removal. The House of Representatives impeached Andrew Johnson in 1868 and William Clinton in 1998. In both cases the Senate voted to acquit. Richard Nixon, on the verge of being impeached, resigned in 1972.

2

1 The House of Representatives impeached Andrew Johnson on the grounds that he violated the 1867 Tenure of Office Act prohibiting the president from removing cabinet members without Senate approval. The law was designed to protect Secretary of War Edwin Stanton, who oversaw the military occupation of the South and implemented Republican Party Reconstruction reforms that Johnson opposed. Johnson dismissed Stanton and, in a highly partisan move, the Republicans in Congress impeached him. The Senate acquitted Johnson by one vote. ∾ This 1868 photo shows the House of Representatives managers of Andrew Johnson's impeachment case. In the Senate, where such a case is tried, House representatives serve as the prosecuting attorneys. (Courtesy Library of Congress)

2 George T. Brown, sergeant-at-arms of the Senate, serving the summons on President Johnson, from *Harper's Weekly*, March 28, 1868. (Courtesy Library of Congress)

3 On July 30, 1974, the Judiciary Committee of the House of Representatives approved three articles of impeachment against Richard Nixon. The committee charged the president with obstruction of justice and misuse of presidential power.

The testimony of high-level White House officials and tape recordings made in the Oval Office revealed a history of break-ins, unauthorized wiretappings, political "dirty tricks," hush-money payments, and wrongful use of the Internal Revenue Service. With little or no support in either political party, Nixon, on August 8, became the only president to resign from office.

∾ These photographs by Fred J. Maroon show the Senate hearings on September 24, 1973, and President Nixon addressing cabinet members and White House staff during his farewell in the East Room on August 9, 1974. His daughter Julie and her husband David Eisenhower are standing behind him. (Courtesy Fred J. Maroon)

3

4

4 On December 18, 1998, the House of Representatives voted to impeach William Clinton. The charges were perjury and obstruction of justice stemming from the president's testimony in a civil suit and whether he lied about a sexual relationship with a White House intern. The debate largely focused on whether his crimes, if real, rose to the level of an impeachable offense. Clinton was acquitted in the Senate of both charges. ∾ The House of Representatives case managers in the impeachment trial of William Clinton.

(Courtesy Congressman James E. Rogan)
∾ This robe was worn by Chief Justice William H. Rehnquist during sessions of the Supreme Court and during the Senate impeachment trial of President William Clinton.

1

WE THE PEOPLE

Presidential power ultimately derives from the people. Getting elected is just the beginning. Only by maintaining public support does an administration sustain its influence. Popular presidents have the ability to promote their policies, pressure members of Congress, and defend against attacks. Conversely, should a president fall sharply in opinion polls, his administration is vulnerable.

1 The actions of the president are closely scrutinized by an enormous press corp. The reporters are always on the lookout for a good story, and no story is better than an overreaching president or a juicy scandal. Keeping a watchful eye on the chief executive, the press helps to curb presidential power that threatens to exceed its legal limits or the public's wishes. ⌁ Veteran White House reporter Helen Thomas questioning President Carter during a press conference. (Courtesy Jimmy Carter Library)

2 Cartoon of Grover Cleveland fishing for popularity, *Puck*, 1886.

2

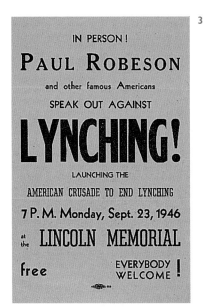

IN PERSON!

PAUL ROBESON

and other famous Americans

SPEAK OUT AGAINST

LYNCHING!

LAUNCHING THE

AMERICAN CRUSADE TO END LYNCHING

7 P. M. Monday, Sept. 23, 1946

at the LINCOLN MEMORIAL

free   EVERYBODY WELCOME!

3

5

4

NOT FOUR MORE YEARS.. NOT ONE MORE DAY.. U.S. OUT NOW!

6

The most essential right of citizens in a free society is the ability to challenge the decisions and actions of their government and to make their opinions known. The First Amendment to the Constitution guarantees the rights to assemble peacefully and petition the government for a redress of grievances. From local protests to marches on Washington, demonstrations have forced presidents to publicly take stands and clarify positions on is-

sues they often wish to avoid.

3 1946 handbill publicizing a Washington demonstration that called for federal anti-lynching legislation. Organizers hoped to put pressure on the President and Congress to address the indifference of local law officials to the lynching of Southern Blacks.

4 Anti-Vietnam War protest sign, about 1973.

5 Veterans protesting on the Capitol steps

during the 1932 Bonus March, in which they demanded early distribution of the cash bonus promised to them for military service in World War I. (Courtesy National Archives)

6 Martin Luther King Jr. and civil rights supporters during the 1963 Civil Rights March on Washington. The march represented the apex of the civil rights movement, as thousands

protested racial discrimination and expressed their support for landmark civil rights legislation that was pending in Congress. (Courtesy National Archives)

1

1 Early Gallup pollsters (Courtesy Gallup Organization)

2 Tabulation of viewing data gleaned from sample homes enabled media specialists to hone or redefine the president's presence on television.

~ The A. C. Nielsen audimeter and film cartridge, along with a viewing diary, measured radio or television use. Devices like this "black box" of the television ratings system gathered data on family listening and viewing habits from 1949 into the 1970s. Connected to a radio or television, they registered set use and station tuning by exposing 16-mm film to a pinpoint of light. When changed by the homeowner on a weekly basis, the film cartridge ejected a quarter to assure timely mailings to the Nielsen Company for analysis.

3 Gallup polls news release (Courtesy Gallup Organization)

4 Toy football devised by the Luntz Research Companies to stimulate focus group discussions of political issues.

5 Gallup pollsters (Courtesy Gallup Organization)

6 Exit-polling sheets from the 1996 New Hampshire presidential primary.

2

PUBLIC OPINION NEWS SERVICE

For Release Friday, Sept. 22

Roosevelt Popularity With Voters Up Sharply Since Outbreak of War, Poll Finds

President Nearly as Strong as When He Was Re-elected in 1936

By DR. GEORGE GALLUP
Director, American Institute of Public Opinion
Copyright, 1939

PRINCETON, N. J., Sept. 21—With Congress and the nation poised on the threshold of a great debate on the neutrality issue, President Roosevelt's popularity with the rank and file of American voters has increased sharply since the outbreak of war in Europe. Coinciding with the President's "limited emergency" moves of the last few weeks and his appeal for national unity, the American Institute's monthly index of Presidential popularity shows a five-point rise since August and finds Roosevelt nearly as popular today as when he was re-elected by a landslide in 1936.

Last month 56.6 per cent of major party voters in an Institute survey approved of Roosevelt as President. Today the figure has jumped to 61.0 per cent. He was re-elected in 1936 with 62.5 per cent.

Throughout the South and Far West—Democratic strongholds—the President's popularity remains about the same as in previous surveys, with slight increases, while in New England opinion is still almost evenly divided. The President's chief gains in the last month have come principally in the industrial Middle Atlantic and East Central states and in the Mid-West farm area. In those places the percentage of voters approving him as President today has jumped from 6 to 10 points.

Approve of Roosevelt as President

	Today	Last Month	Points Change
New England	53%	51%	+2
Middle Atlantic	58	54	+4
East Central	59	51	+8
West Central	60	55	+5
South	72	70	+2
Far West	65	64	+1

A question which remains to be answered is whether the increase in support for Roosevelt's present policies will have an important effect on third term sentiment. Last month's survey found that whereas 56.6 per cent approved of Roosevelt as President at that time, only 40 per cent said they would vote for him if he ran for a third term. A survey which will show the trend of third term sentiment since the outbreak of war is now being completed by the Institute.

Foreign Crises

Aid Popularity

ONE probable explanation for the sudden spurt in Presidential support is that the Administration's foreign policy has been one of the most popular policies of the whole New Deal. Institute studies have found that whereas the rank and file of Democrats and Republicans disagree sharply on many vital domestic issues, they are in substantial agreement over foreign policy. And in the last few weeks, foreign policy has occupied so much public attention that domestic issues, with their concomitant divisions of opinion, have been largely thrust aside.

However, the rise in Roosevelt's popularity should cause no surprise to students who in the past have observed the effect of foreign crises on the prestige of the Administration. At the time of the Sudeten crisis in 1938, when Roosevelt sent peace pleas to Hitler and Mussolini, his popularity rose six points in less than a month.

Intensity of Feeling Is Measured

BESIDES indicating the number of voters who approve or disapprove of Roosevelt at the present time, today's survey attempted to measure the intensity of pro-Roosevelt and anti-Roosevelt sentiment. It inquired of all voters whether they approved "strongly" or "mildly" or disapproved "strongly" or "mildly." The results showed that the "strongly approve" outweighed the "strongly disapprove," indicating a greater intensity favorable to the President than unfavorable.

Approve Strongly	
Approve Mildly	
Disapprove Strongly	
Disapprove Mildly	

3

TALK TO ME

4

5

TAKING THE PUBLIC'S PULSE

Presidents have historically used a variety of techniques to measure public opinion. In the early part of the twentieth century, presidents relied on informal reports from party activists, the news media, and their own political instincts to gauge public opinion. By the 1930s, professional pollsters such as George Gallup and, later, focus groups started to replace those methods. Today, computers and sophisticated software programs are used to measure the popularity of the president's programs. Although some presidents have been criticized for pandering to opinion polls, those who ignore public sentiment risk the effectiveness of their administrations.

6

3

1 Sign with caricature of Carter, and photograph from a farmers' protest in Washington, D.C., 1978.

2 Protest buttons.

3 Demonstration in front of the White House as President Bush announces the beginning of the Gulf War.

4 Protest poster from Washington, D.C., antiabortion march, 1992.

5 "Whose Streets/Our Streets" poster from the mass protests held at the World Bank and International Monetary Fund, Washington, D.C., April 2000. Protesters opposed President Clinton's support of World Trade Organization and International Monetary Fund trade policies, accusing the organizations of favoring commercial interests over environmental and human rights concerns. During the protest, activists complained about police harassment and defended their right to demonstrate.

5

4

THE WHITE HOUSE AS SYMBOL AND HOME

It has 132 rooms, 32 bathrooms, 412 doors, 147 windows, 28 fireplaces, 7 staircases, and 3 elevators. It was burned by the British in 1814 and survived a fire in 1929. It has been renovated, gutted, and endlessly remodeled to suit the fancy of every president and first lady. ❧ As the oldest, continuously occupied official residence of a chief of state in the western world, the White House reflects the president's overlapping role as head of state, head of government, and head of a family. It is where the president greets visiting dignitaries, attends state dinners, and holds press conferences. It is Buckingham Palace and Number 10 Downing Street rolled into one. It is where the president and his family live and play with the first pet. This melding of public and private space has shaped the lives of everyone who has ever called the White House home. ❧ It hasn't always been called the White House. At various points in its history

OPPOSITE: Lucy Webb Hayes with two of her children and a family friend in the White House conservatory, 1879. (Courtesy Rutherford B. Hayes Presidential Center)

Painted wood dinner favor from a White House dinner during the administration of Benjamin Harrison (1889–93).

this grand building has been known as the "President's Palace," the "President's House," and the "Executive Mansion." Theodore Roosevelt officially named it the White House in 1902.

One hundred and two years earlier, John Adams and his wife, Abigail, became the first occupants of the new home. Since then each president and first lady have made changes and additions to the building. Running water was added in 1833, central heating in 1837, gaslights in 1848, an elevator in 1882, and electricity in 1891. When Theodore Roosevelt and his family moved in, he found the White House too small to accommodate his six children as well as the growing office needs of the presidency. Roosevelt tapped Charles McKim, one of the leading architects of the day, to undertake the first major remodeling of the White House in a hundred years. Additional renovations changed the White House in the years that followed.

By the time President Truman took office, however, the White House had become a firetrap, crisscrossed with old dry wood and

Charred timber found during the 1948–52 Truman administration renovation of the White House. The wood is believed to have survived from 1814, when the British burned the building during James Madison's presidency.

crumbling mortar. When the leg of Margaret Truman's piano sank between two floorboards and into the plaster ceiling below, Truman retreated to Blair House, and ordered a complete reconstruction. Between 1948 and 1952 workmen gutted most of the interior and built a new White House inside the shell of the old.

Subsequent first families have continued to alter the private areas of the White House to suit their tastes and preferences. But one thing has proven impervious to change: the first family's struggle to live a "normal," private life in this most public of buildings.

The White House is a fishbowl, whose occupants live under close and continuous scrutiny. People want to know what the president and his family are wearing, eating, and reading. They want to know who was born, who died, who got married, and who's ill. The home is constantly filled with people: secretaries, aides and interns, cooks, waiters, chiefs of staff, reporters, secret service agents, high-ranking politicians, military brass, international statesmen, and distinguished citizens—all wanting a moment with the president and his family, all wanting a piece of their privacy, and all believing that the concerns of the state outweigh the needs of the family. Such is the price of living at America's most famous address.

No one knew this better than Harry Truman. Of his years in the White House, Truman lamented: "It seems like there was always somebody for dinner."

Program and menu for a White House dinner given by Theodore Roosevelt for Prince Henry of Prussia, 1902.

Bill Clinton's high school tenor saxophone made by C. G. Conn Ltd., Elkhardt, Indiana. (Lent by President Bill Clinton)

Coins collected by Dwight Eisenhower.

BUILDING THE FIRST WHITE HOUSE

WASHINGTON D.C. 1798

1 Aerial view of the White House. (Courtesy Library of Congress)
2 President George Washington inspecting the unfinished White House with architect James Hoban.
〰 Photolithograph based on a twentieth-century painting by N. C. Wyeth.
3 *State Dining Room at Christmas* by Thomas

William Jones was the cover illustration of Ronald Reagan's 1987 Hallmark Christmas card.
4 President Warren G. Harding wore these elegant silk pajamas made by Chavert & Fils, Inc., of New York and Paris. His monogram is embroidered on the left pocket.

I don't know whether it's the finest public housing in America or the crown jewel of prison life. It's a very isolating life.

William Jefferson Clinton

THE WHITE HOUSE AS SYMBOL AND HOME

Symbolically the White House embodies the principles of our democratic form of government, a government in which the elected representatives of the people lead lives that are roughly similar to those they represent. In keeping with that democratic tradition, the president and his family live in a house, not a palace.

Yet the White House is no ordinary house. A shrine to democracy, a sprawling office complex, and a historic home, it serves many functions that place a unique burden on its occupants. Always in the public eye, the first family must remain accessible to the American people. Yet they must also have time and space to escape from the pressures and scrutiny of office. Balancing their public and private lives has proved one of the greatest challenges facing the individuals who live at 1600 Pennsylvania Avenue.

3

BUILDING THE WHITE HOUSE

The first residents of the White House, John and Abigail Adams, moved into the incomplete building in late 1800. Only six of the thirty rooms were habitable. Wind and rain seeped in, and a ceiling in one of the main rooms collapsed shortly after they arrived. There were no fences around the building, and the yard was strewn with workmen's shanties and loose bricks. Despite these hardships, Abigail Adams set to work making the new president's house livable, setting up a drawing room to entertain guests.

The White House has changed drastically since the Adamses moved in. Coat after coat of paint, layers of wallpaper, and new carpeting changed the look of the interior. New portraits and pictures were hung on walls. Holes were punched in the walls to add new pipes and wiring. Offices were built, rebuilt, and reshuffled to accommodate the president's staff and their typewriters, telegraphs, telephones, and computers. East and West wings were added. This legacy of change will likely continue in the twenty-first century as the White House is renovated to suit the needs of the presidency and the tastes of the first family.

4

1

1 A Maypole celebra-
tion during the Herbert
Hoover administration
in the early 1930s.
(Courtesy Library of
Congress)
2 President Lyndon
Johnson and Vice Presi-
dent Hubert Humphrey
greeting tourists
through the White
House fence, 1965.
(Courtesy Lyndon
Baines Johnson Library)
3 Gerald and Betty
Ford in front of the tree
at the Christmas ball for
members of Congress,
1974. (Courtesy Gerald

R. Ford Library)
4 In 1975, Betty Ford's
Christmas greeting to
the public included in-
structions for making
ornaments from folk art
materials, such as this
pig from the Fords'
Christmas tree that year.
5 President Johnson
birthday greetings.
6 Wooden Easter eggs:
George Bush, 1989, and
Ronald Reagan, 1988
(Lent by Daniel, Katie,
and Sarah Chew); Bill
Clinton, 1996. (Lent by
Katie and Sarah Bunch)

OPEN TO THE PUBLIC

Presidents create events that encourage people to feel they have access to the leader of a democratic society. Thomas Jefferson opened
the lawn around the White House in celebration of the Fourth of
July. In the 1840s the tradition of musical concerts gained popularity, attracting large crowds in subsequent years. First families have
hosted public celebrations that include the Easter egg roll, Christmas tree lightings, receptions, and picnics.

These events symbolize the unique relationship between our
chief elected official and the voters he serves. No president can afford to appear aloof or distant from the public.

Nobody ever drops in for the evening. William Howard Taft

OFFICIAL OCCASIONS

As the nation's official hosts, the president and his family are responsible for receiving a wide variety of dignitaries at the White House. Over the years visitors have ranged from members of the Osage Indian tribe to representatives from the People's Republic of China.

The format for these meetings varies from receptions and closed-door meetings to balls and state dinners. Important personal relationships and significant decisions can emerge from such gatherings. The challenge is to use the occasions effectively.

One of the White House's most stylish and popular hostesses, Grace Coolidge wore this chiffon velvet "flapper-style" evening dress during her husband's administration (1923–29). The dress has a detachable train and matching velvet shoes with rhinestone buckles (not shown).

6

7

1 This Sèvres gravy boat is from a set of personal china purchased in France by John and Abigail Adams.

2 Dessert plate from a French service used by James and Elizabeth Monroe. The service represents the first official White House china to incorporate a design. The arms of the United States are in the center and the border designs represent strength, art, commerce, science, and agriculture. The service was ordered by Monroe in 1817 and was made in Paris at the Pierre Louis Dagoty and Edouard D. Honoré factory.

3 This game plate, "The Woodcock," is part of the Rutherford and Lucy Hayes state china, manufactured by Haviland Company in

1880. Their service was designed by Theodore Russell Davis, an artist and reporter for *Harper's Weekly*. The unique china is decorated with nature scenes and a variety of American plants, birds, and animals.

4 Lady Bird Johnson oversaw the design of state china ordered during her husband's administration (1963–69). The china showcases the wildflowers of North America. Each plate in the dessert service is hand-painted with the official flower of one of the states or the District of Columbia. This plate shows the American Beauty rose, the official flower of the District of Columbia. It was designed by Tiffany & Co. and manufactured by Castleton China, Inc.

5 First Lady Nancy Reagan used private funds to pay for this service, designed and manufactured by Lenox in 1981. The cost of reportedly more than $200,000 generated some controversy.

6 James Buchanan greeting envoys from Japan, 1860. (Courtesy Library of Congress)

7 Ronald and Nancy Reagan hosting a state dinner in 1981 for Australian Prime Minister Malcolm Fraser. (Courtesy Ronald Reagan Library)

8 Menu, printed in English and Chinese, from the state dinner given by Jimmy Carter for Vice Premier Deng Xiaoping of the People's Republic of China and Madame Zhuo Lin on January 29, 1979.

8

宴会

海鲜百花卷
烧烤小牛腿
並红花香饭 翡翠甘兰花
生拌苣荬西洋芥
计司
奶油栗子冻
巧克力点心
咖啡

白宫
一九七九年一月廿九日

DINNER

Paul
Masson
Pinot
Chardonnay   Timbale of Seafood
1976   Fleurons

Simi
Rosé   Roast Stuffed Loin of Veal
Cabernet   Saffron Rice
Sauvignon
1976   Broccoli Spears

Endive and Watercress Salad
Hanns
Kornell   Trappist Cheese
Champagne

Chestnut Mousse
Chocolate Truffles

Demitasse

THE WHITE HOUSE
Monday, January 29, 1979

1

2

3

WHITE HOUSE WEDDINGS

Maria Monroe was the first daughter of a president to get married in the White House, in 1820. Her ceremony was restricted to family only. Subsequent weddings have become increasingly popular events. The public wants to know what the bride is wearing, how the house is decorated, how the invitations are worded, the honeymoon plans, and many other details.

More recent White House brides have resorted to elaborate schemes to maintain a semblance of privacy. In 1966 Luci Johnson somehow managed to keep her dress design secret until the day of her wedding.

1 Grover Cleveland was the first president to be married in the White House. He married Frances Folsom in a private ceremony held on June 2, 1886. Their wedding announcement was sent the next day.

~ Frances Folsom

Cleveland gave this wedding picture to family only. (Courtesy Library of Congress)

~ Satin-covered cake boxes, trimmed with lace, were given to wedding guests.

~ Box, *right*, given to Reverend Byron Sunder-

land, who officiated at the private White House ceremony.

2 Alice Roosevelt Longworth flanked by her husband Nicholas Longworth and her father President Theodore Roosevelt, on her wedding day, February 17,

1906. (Courtesy Library of Congress)

3 Jessie, President Wilson's daughter, married Francis Sayre on November 25, 1913. (Courtesy Culver Pictures)

116

4

4 Luci Baines Johnson Nugent tossing her wedding bouquet, August 6, 1966.
5 Tricia Nixon at her wedding with her parents and her husband, Edward Cox, June 12, 1971. (Courtesy Richard Nixon Birthplace and Library)

5

Franklin D. Roosevelt's grandchildren having a snowball fight on the White House lawn, 1939. (Courtesy Bettmann/Corbis)

1

2

3

4

5

6

1 Wooden paint box used by Archie Roosevelt, son of Theodore Roosevelt, around 1903. Made in France, the paintbox includes paints, charcoals, chalk, mixing cups and trays, and copper stencils. The lid, découpaged with a design of birds reading a book, has Archie's name written on it.

2 Baseball pass presented to President Harding by the National League of Professional Baseball Clubs in 1921. The pass "extends the courtesy of all its grounds to the Hon. Warren G. Harding and Party."

3 John Quincy Adams' granddaughter, Mary Louisa Adams, was the first child born in the White House. This doll, "Sally," made for her by her aunt Mrs. Thomas Boylston Adams, is cloth-bodied with a bisque head.

4 Dollhouse made by a White House gardener for the children of Grover Cleveland during his second administration. The hinged front of the dollhouse swings open to reveal two floors of five rooms, all with electricity.

5 Rosalynn and Amy Carter relaxing at the White House, 1979. (Courtesy Jimmy Carter Library)

6 John F. Kennedy in the Oval Office, with his son John playing under his desk, May 25, 1962. (Photograph by Stanley Tretick. Courtesy Bettmann/Corbis)

7 This "Imperial" deep sea fishing reel was said to be a great favorite of Herbert Hoover's. Hoover's initials are scratched into the side.

CREATING A PRIVATE LIFE

When George Washington took office, he decided that the president should work and live in the same residence. Every chief executive since has abided by that rule and while it makes performing the job of president more efficient, it also makes family life more difficult. Quiet time and family privacy must be snatched from or interwoven with official business.

7

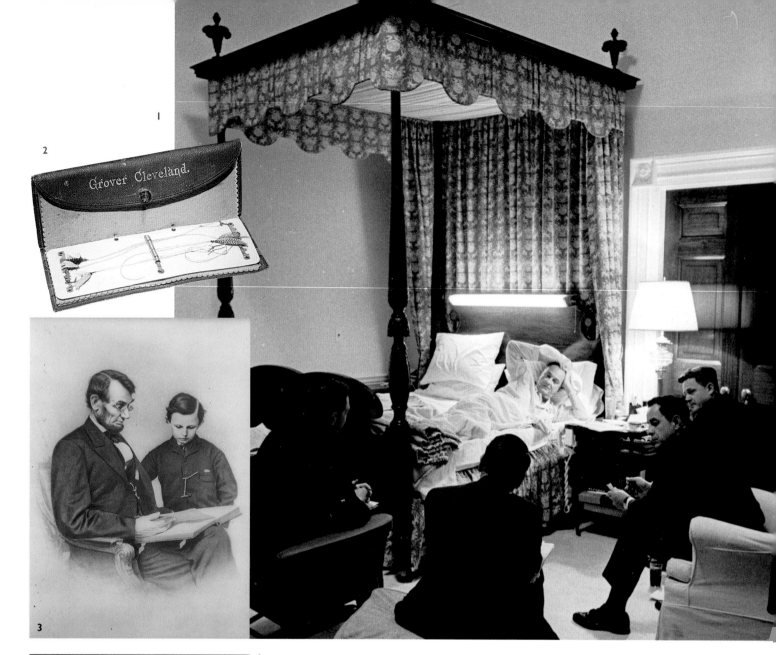

1 Lyndon Johnson in his bedroom talking with members of his staff, 1966. (Courtesy Lyndon Baines Johnson Library)

2 Trout flies in a leather case belonging to Grover Cleveland.

3 Abraham Lincoln with his son Tad (Thomas), 1864. (Courtesy Library of Congress)

4 Woodrow Wilson holding his first granddaughter, Ellen Wilson McAdoo, 1915. (Courtesy Library of Congress)

5 Franklin D. Roosevelt with his popular dog, Fala, 1940. (Courtesy Bettman/Corbis)

6 First Lady Grace Coolidge with her pet raccoon, early 1920s. (Courtesy Library of Congress)

7 Wooden bowling pin used in the White House during Harry Truman's administration. Truman installed the original bowling alley in the White House in 1947.

8 Harry Truman's Royal Palm Sports Wear shirt was made in Miami, Florida, and he wore it there at the Little White House in 1948. The president gave this shirt to his friend, who teased him about his loud attire. It is autographed by the Truman family.

5

6

8

I may be President of the
United States, but my private life
is nobody's business. Chester A. Arthur

7

ASSASSINATION AND MOURNING

Millions of Americans remember exactly where they were on November 22, 1963, the day John F. Kennedy was assassinated in Dallas, Texas. They remember the shock and disbelief that accompanied the announcement of his death. They recall the public stoicism and grief of the Kennedy family: how the country's desire to share its sorrow forced the family to sacrifice their privacy to address this public need. They will never forget the long funeral caravan, accompanied by the flag-draped caisson, muffled drums, and a riderless horse with the backward boot in the stirrup, slowly, almost painfully, winding its way through the streets of the nation's capital. And they think back to the discussions surrounding a permanent and appropriately public final resting place. What most Americans did not realize was that the ceremonies and memorialization that are so central to our memories about the death of President Kennedy

OPPOSITE: President John F. Kennedy lying in state. (Courtesy Bettmann/Corbis)

This is one of four drums that played a muffled cadence during the funeral procession of John F. Kennedy. (Lent by U. S. Department of Defense, Department of the Army)

were really part of a long tradition of ritualized mourning, with an attendant period of national questioning and reflection, that harks back to the assassination of Abraham Lincoln.

The sudden death of the president of the United States, especially by assassination, is a traumatic moment that shocks the nation and elicits a sense of crisis that frequently eroded America's certitude in its moral and political values. Too often, as one mourner commented after the assassination of William McKinley, "we are left sitting in the dark, still wondering how such a deed could have been done . . . in fair and free America." Concern for the safety of the man who holds the nation's highest office has been a significant consideration at least since the attempted assassination of Andrew Jackson in 1835. There have been countless threats and eleven publicly acknowledged attempts on the lives of the presidents, four of whom—Abraham Lincoln, James Garfield, William McKinley, and John F. Kennedy—have died from assassins' bullets. Sadly, in a democratic nation that demands access to and accountability from its elected leaders, presidents are vulnerable. As the central political and national leader, the American president becomes a symbol not just for all that is good about America but also for all that is wrong, incomplete, unfair, and unaddressed— whether real or imagined. The threat of assassination is little mentioned or rarely acknowledged publicly by America's presidents. For some, there was little to gain from dwelling on a possibility that could hinder their ability to lead. Others would concur with Harry Truman's words shortly after an attack on his life in 1950, "a president has to expect those things."

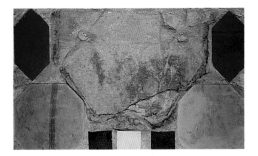

When President Garfield was assassinated on July 2, 1881, legend suggests that his body fell on this section of tile taken from the Baltimore & Potomac Railroad station. Much like the assassination of Abraham Lincoln, the death of Garfield led many Americans to find, buy, or otherwise obtain some material reminder of the president. This object was donated to the Smithsonian Institution in 1909 by James Garfield, son of the president.

The United States Secret Service was entrusted with ensuring the safety of the president in 1901, shortly after the assassination of William McKinley. Created in 1865 to safeguard the nation's currency, the Secret Service has protected every American president elected in the twentieth century, from Theodore Roosevelt to William Clinton. Although the president will always remain a visible, and thereby, vulnerable symbol of America, he is able to perform the duties of his office, due in part to the creativity and courage of the men and women of the United States Secret Service, whose job is "simply" to protect the president.

When a president dies in office either from assassination or natural causes, a grieving nation has needs and expectations. To meet these demands, a series of governmental traditions, mourning rituals, and practices of official remembrances has evolved over the two-hundred-year history of the presidency. Combining military customs, partisan political considerations, Victorian era funeral practices, and religious doctrine, the manner in which America mourns its highest elected official provides for both public and familial expressions of grief. One of the goals of these activities was to create opportunities for the widest array of Americans to express publicly their feelings of loss. Beginning with the death of Lincoln, the remains would lie in state, usually in the Capitol rotunda, and then travel by train to a number of cities where each, through funeral processionals and public programs, would honor the martyred president and eventually be laid to rest in his hometown (a notable exception was President Kennedy, who was buried in Arlington National Cemetery). Before the advent of television, this was the most efficient manner to ensure wide public participation during the period of mourning. Equally important was the need to create a ceremony that befit America's growing international stature and one that would also convey a sense of political and domestic stability. To many, the greatest comforts that these activities provided were a demonstration of the peaceful and constitutional transference of power and a renewed confidence in the strength and perseverance of the American political system.

On September 6, 1881, President Garfield was transported by train from Washington to the beachfront home of Charles Francklyn in Long Branch, New Jersey. To ease the strain on the president, a special spur line was built directly to the house where he would reside. Spikes from that spur became valued souvenirs sold to a public desperate for any tangible remembrance of their fallen leader.

1

If it is [God's] will that I must die at the hand of an assassin, I must be resigned. I must do my duty as I see it, and leave the rest with God. — Abraham Lincoln, 1864

THE DEATH OF ABRAHAM LINCOLN

The first American president to be assassinated was attacked by John Wilkes Booth, a Southern sympathizer, at Ford's Theatre on April 14, 1865, five days after the end of the Civil War. In death, Lincoln achieved the adoration and popular appeal that eluded him in life. He became a martyr for national unity and equality and a hero to the millions who responded to his death with an unprecedented outpouring of grief. The manner in which America mourned Lincoln evolved into rituals that shaped the way the country reacted to future tragedies, including John F. Kennedy's assassination a hundred years later.

2

1 "Columbia Grieving at Lincoln's Bier," from *Harper's Weekly*, April 29, 1865. Images such as this, printed in nearly every newspaper throughout America, reflected the depth of the nation's grief over the assassination of Lincoln. (Courtesy Smithsonian Institution Libraries)

2 Drum and drumsticks played at Lincoln's funeral.

3 Objects owned by or associated with Lincoln quickly became relics, reminding Americans of Lincoln's greatness and challenging them to keep his ideals alive.
∾ This sleeve cuff purportedly bearing Lincoln's blood was worn by Laura Keene, the star of the Ford Theatre's production of *Our American Cousin.* According to legend, Keene rushed to Lincoln's box to bring water to the wounded president. Cradling Lincoln's head as he drank, her cuff became marked with a trace of his blood.

4 One of the Smithsonian Institution's most treasured icons is this top hat, worn by Lincoln to Ford's Theatre on the night of his assassination.

5 The public had an insatiable appetite for visual representations, like this newspaper illustration, of the assassination of Lincoln. (Courtesy Library of Congress)

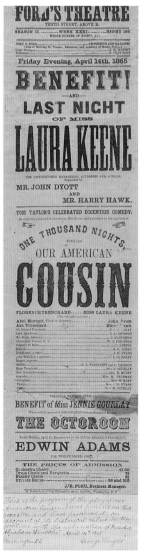

"OH THAT MOURNFUL NIGHT": THE ASSASSINATION OF ABRAHAM LINCOLN

On April 14, 1865, President and Mrs. Lincoln planned to go to Ford's Theatre with General and Mrs. Grant. The Grants decided not to come and their place was taken by Clara Harris and her fiancé, Henry Rathbone.

At 10:15, as the audience roared with laughter at the climactic line ("You sockdologizing old mantrap"), actor John Wilkes Booth shot Lincoln and severely wounded Rathbone with a knife. Witnesses claimed that Booth cried either "Sic semper tyrannis" (Thus be it ever to tyrants) or "The South shall be free." Despite breaking a leg as he leaped onto the stage during his getaway, Booth mounted a waiting horse and escaped into southern Maryland.

Lincoln was taken to a house across from the theater where he died the next morning.

1 Ford's Theatre, site of the assassination of Abraham Lincoln, is on 10th Street between E and F Streets in Washington, D.C. It was built in 1863. (Courtesy Library of Congress)

2 *National Police Gazette,* April 22, 1865, dramatizing the assassination of President Lincoln and the attempted assassination of Secretary of State William H. Seward.

3 Ticket and playbill to the Ford's Theatre production of *Our American Cousin,* starring Laura Keene, for April 14, 1865, the night Abraham Lincoln was assassinated.

I struck for my country and that alone.

John Wilkes Booth, April 21, 1865

4 The Lincoln conspirators. (Courtesy Library
of Congress)
5 For twelve days, John
Wilkes Booth avoided
capture. The govern-
ment offered significant
rewards for any informa-
tion that would lead to
the capture of the assas-
sins. (Courtesy Library
of Congress)
6 Once captured, the
Lincoln conspirators
were closely and con-
stantly guarded. During
their trial, iron keys

locked their prison cells.
The nation's emotions
were so strong that the
Lincoln conspirators,
except for the lone fe-
male prisoner, Mary
Surratt, were bound
even during the trial.
These ankle shackles
confined the defendants.
7 Prison hoods worn by
defendents in their cells
and as they were trans-
ported to the trial.

THE ASSASSINS

Booth's attack on the president was part of a plan to improve
chances for a separate Southern nation by murdering influential
members of the government including Lincoln, Vice President
Andrew Johnson, Secretary of State William Seward, and General
Ulysses S. Grant. (Seward was also wounded on that night, but
Johnson and Grant escaped harm.) Had the plan succeeded, Booth
thought the resulting chaos would force the North to accept a
negotiated peace that would preserve the Confederacy.

Booth and at least nine other Southern sympathizers were the
subjects of an intensive manhunt. Booth was located on a south-
eastern Virginia farm on April 26, and died from wounds incurred
during his capture. The others were tried in a military court. Four
were hanged that July. Four received prison sentences (commuted
by Andrew Johnson in 1869). Only one conspirator escaped prison
when the jury was unable to reach a verdict during his 1867 trial.

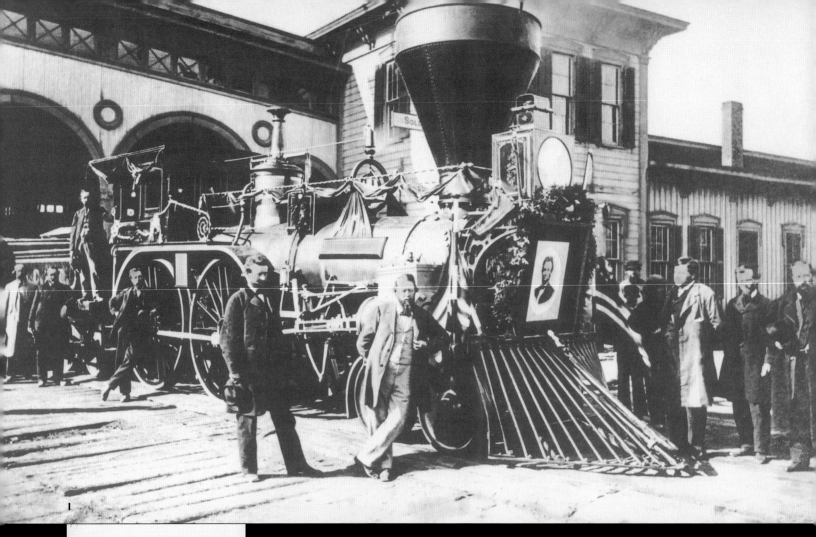

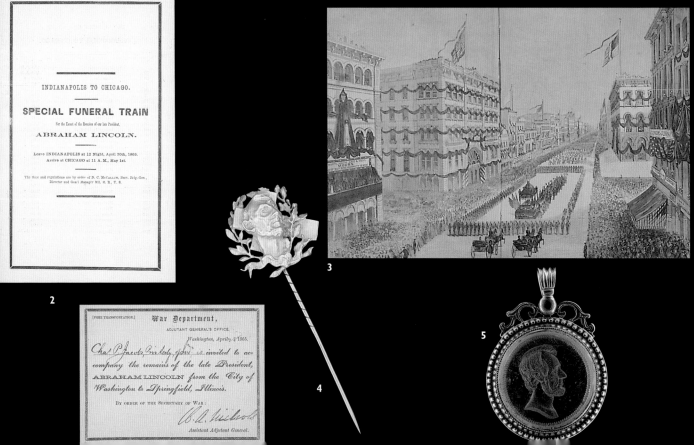

INDIANAPOLIS TO CHICAGO.

SPECIAL FUNERAL TRAIN

For the Escort of the Remains of our late President,

ABRAHAM LINCOLN.

Leave INDIANAPOLIS at 12 Night, April 30th, 1865.
Arrive at CHICAGO at 11 A. M., May 1st.

The time and regulations are by order of D. C. McCallum, Bret. Brig.-Gen.,
Director and Gen'l Manager Mil. R. R., U. S.

2

3

[FREE TRANSPORTATION.]
War Department,
ADJUTANT GENERAL'S OFFICE.
Washington, April 2, 1865.

Chas P Jacob, cordially, you is invited to ac-
company the remains of the late President,
ABRAHAM LINCOLN from the City of
Washington to Springfield, Illinois.

BY ORDER OF THE SECRETARY OF WAR:

Assistant Adjutant General.

4

5

THE LONG AND FINAL RIDE: THE FUNERAL OF ABRAHAM LINCOLN

Some wanted Lincoln to remain in Washington, but Mary Lincoln decided he should be buried in Springfield, Illinois, his former home. Before leaving Washington on April 21, Lincoln lay in state in the East Room of the White House. Then, after a two-hour funeral processional that included thousands of soldiers, politicians, diplomats, and newly freed slaves, he was placed in the Capitol rotunda.

To allow the nation to mourn, Lincoln's body retraced the train route taken by the president-elect in 1861 through Baltimore, Philadelphia, New York, and Chicago. In each city, parades were held with caissons, riderless horses, and an array of elected officials. Businesses closed; eulogies were delivered. Not until May 4 was Lincoln buried. His train did not just transport him to Illinois, "it transported [Lincoln] to immortality."

PERSONAL MOURNING

Lincoln was assassinated on Good Friday. That enabled many to find a spiritual and personal connection to his death. Some viewed Lincoln's murder as an atonement for the sins of the nation after years of war and bitterness. Writers like Walt Whitman and Ralph Waldo Emerson expressed their pain and admiration in poetry and prose. Countless Americans wore pins, lockets, badges, and rings as public expressions of mourning and memory.

1 For nearly two weeks, from April 21 to May 3, this train carried the body of Abraham Lincoln home to Springfield, Illinois. (Courtesy Library of Congress) 2 The Lincoln funeral train had eight coaches: six to carry the invited mourners, one for the military honor guard, and one with the body.

Those asked to ride this train received special invitations and timetables. 3 Lincoln's funeral train arrived in New York City on Monday, April 23, 1865. This image from *Harper's Weekly* captures the nation's largest city in mourning. (Courtesy Smithsonian Institution Libraries) 4 This mourning scarf

pin belonged to Mary Todd Lincoln, the widow of the president. 5 Mourning locket with the inscription, "Born Feb. 12, 1809. Assassinated April 14, 1865." 6 One of two vases placed beside the body of Abraham Lincoln at his funeral.

> We are left sitting in the dark, still wondering how such a deed could have been done . . . in a free and fair America.

Unidentified mourner at the funeral of William McKinley

1 Richard Lawrence, an unemployed house painter, tried to kill President Andrew Jackson in 1835 in order to redress imagined slights. This print, created twenty years after the assassination attempt, was made from a sketch by an eyewitness. It became quite popular because it shows the aging president boldly confronting his attacker. (Courtesy Library of Congress)
2 Telephone inventor Alexander Graham Bell using his "induction balance" in an unsuccessful attempt to find the bullet that would eventually kill President

Garfield. From *Harper's Weekly,* August 13, 1881. (Courtesy Library of Congress)
3 The White House draped in mourning shortly after the death of James Garfield on September 19, 1881. (Courtesy Rutherford B. Hayes Presidential Center)
4 Theodore Roosevelt survived an attempted assassination when the bullet was deflected and slowed by his metal eyeglass case and by a folded fifty-page speech. This first page of the address was held aloft for the audience to see the hole caused by the bullet.

THE ATTACK ON ANDREW JACKSON

On January 30, 1835, President Andrew Jackson attended a congressional funeral in the Capitol building. As he exited, Richard Lawrence, an unemployed house painter, pointed a pistol at Jackson and fired. The percussion cap exploded, but the bullet did not discharge. The enraged Jackson raised his cane to throttle his attacker, who fired a second weapon. It also misfired and the 67-year-old president was not hurt.

The deranged Lawrence believed Jackson had conspired to keep him poor and out of work. Jackson was convinced that Lawrence was hired by his political enemies, the Whigs, to stop his plan to destroy the Bank of the United States. Lawrence spent the rest of his life in jails and asylums.

THE DEATH OF JAMES GARFIELD

When James Garfield was attacked on July 2, 1881, the nation was shocked, enraged, and captivated. President for just four months, Garfield was shot by Charles Guiteau as he was about to board a train at the Baltimore & Potomac Railroad station in Washington. Severely wounded, Garfield lingered until September 19.

An unsuccessful lawyer, evangelist, and insurance salesman, Guiteau believed Garfield owed him a patronage position in the diplomatic corps, and that the president's political decisions threatened to destroy the Republican Party. Guiteau was convicted of murder and hanged on June 30, 1882. In 1883 Congress passed the Pendleton Act; it sought to reform civil service and limit the number of patronage seekers like Charles Guiteau.

THE DEATH OF WILLIAM McKINLEY

On September 6, 1901, President William McKinley traveled to Buffalo, New York, to take part in the Pan American Exposition. During an afternoon reception at the Temple of Music, McKinley was shot by Leon Czolgosz, who had waited patiently in a long line of well-wishers who wanted to greet the president. Seriously wounded, McKinley died eight days later on September 14, 1901. Czolgosz—a self proclaimed anarchist—was quickly tried and executed.

> It takes more than that
> to kill a bull moose.

Theodore Roosevelt, 1912 campaign address,
after surviving an attempted assassination

THE ATTEMPTED ASSASSINATION OF THEODORE ROOSEVELT

Theodore Roosevelt, the first president to receive Secret Service protection, lost it after leaving office, even when he ran again for president in 1912 as the candidate of the Progressive Party, popularly called the Bull Moose Party.

Roosevelt was wounded by John Schrank on his way to a campaign appearance at the Milwaukee Auditorium on October 14, 1912. Schrank believed he must kill Roosevelt in order to prevent him from becoming the first American to serve three presidential terms, and because he dreamed that Roosevelt was responsible for the assassination of William McKinley.

Roosevelt was not severely hurt because the bullet struck a metal eyeglass case and was slowed by the fifty-page speech folded in his breast pocket. Despite his wound, Roosevelt delivered his address.

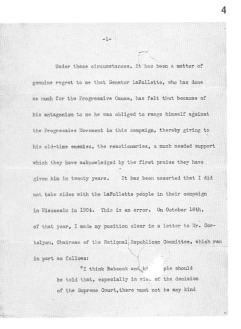

-1-

Under these circumstances, it has been a matter of genuine regret to me that Senator LaFollette, who has done so much for the Progressive Cause, has felt that because of his antagonism to me he was obliged to range himself against the Progressive Movement in this campaign, thereby giving to his old-time enemies, the reactionaries, a much needed support which they have acknowledged by the first praise they have given him in twenty years. It has been asserted that I did not take sides with the LaFollette people in their campaign in Wisconsin in 1904. This is an error. On October 16th, of that year, I made my position clear in a letter to Mr. Cortelyou, Chairman of the National Republican Committee, which ran in part as follows:

"I think Babcock and h[is] [peo]ple should be told that, especially in vie[w] of the decision of the Supreme Court, there must not be any kind

1

2

THE SUDDEN DEATH OF FDR

Franklin D. Roosevelt held the office of president longer than anyone, more than twelve years. Under his direction, the United States endured two of its most significant and overwhelming crises: the Great Depression and World War II. The nation had grown used to Roosevelt's leadership and was comforted by his presence, thanks in part to the strategic use of radio and his "fireside chats." So when Roosevelt died suddenly at Warm Springs, Georgia, on April 12, 1945, Americans were devastated.

3

An assassin's bullet has thrust upon me the awesome burden of the Presidency. I am here to say that I need the help of all Americans, in all America.

Lyndon Baines Johnson

THE LOSS OF JOHN F. KENNEDY

The assassination of John F. Kennedy on November 22, 1963, shocked the nation. Huddled around their television sets, Americans were transfixed by news reports that brought the events of that day and the difficult days that followed directly into their homes. Four decades later, those televised images are still seared in our national memory: the chaos outside Parkland hospital, the shooting of presidential assassin Lee Harvey Oswald, and the bittersweet picture of a young John Kennedy Jr. saluting at his father's funeral.

Kennedy's death ended the optimism that emanated from the youth and idealism of his administration. As the nation mourned, the Kennedy family turned in part to the rituals of official remembrance first practiced after the assassination of Abraham Lincoln.

1-2 Mourners lined the streets of Washington, D.C., as the Roosevelt funeral procession passed. (Courtesy Library of Congress)
3 Many of the public's memories about the Kennedy assassination stem from visual images of the event, like this photograph of the Kennedy family leaving the Capitol on November 24, 1963. (Courtesy Bettmann/Corbis)

135

A president has to expect those things.

Harry S. Truman, shortly after the attack on his life in 1950

Before Theodore Roosevelt's administration, presidential safety was an ad hoc mix of private security, local officers, and presidential confidants. The protection of William McKinley, who received this threatening note while on an 1897 Midwest trip, was handled, quite effectively, by William Williams, director of public safety in Columbus, Ohio. When McKinley was assassinated four years later in Buffalo, New York, the Secret Service formally became the protector of the president.

PROTECTING THE PRESIDENT: THE UNITED STATES SECRET SERVICE

Highly trained and motivated, the special agents and uniformed officers of the United States Secret Service are charged with protecting the president and his family, presidential candidates, and former presidents and with guarding executive offices and diplomatic missions in the capital. After President Kennedy's death in 1963, the agency increased the number of agents detailed to the president, employed new security and communications technology more effectively, and became more proactive in intelligence gathering.

LIKE A CLAP OF THUNDER: ASSASSINATION ATTEMPTS AND THE SUDDEN DEATH OF THE PRESIDENT

In a democracy that demands access to and accountability from its elected leaders, presidents are vulnerable. There have been eleven attempts to kill the president of the United States. Four presidents have died at the hands of an assassin.

In the twentieth century this vulnerability has been greatly reduced by the courage, creativity, and dedication of the United States Secret Service, the agency charged with protecting the president.

Year	President	Assassin	Result
1835	Andrew Jackson	Richard Lawrence	Jackson is unhurt
1865	Abraham Lincoln	John Wilkes Booth	Lincoln is killed
1881	James Garfield	Charles Guiteau	Garfield is killed
1901	William McKinley	Leon Czolgosz	McKinley is killed
1912	Theodore Roosevelt	John Schrank	Roosevelt is wounded
1933	Franklin D. Roosevelt	Giuseppe Zangara	Roosevelt is unhurt
1950	Harry S. Truman	Oscar Collazo	Truman is unhurt
		Griselio Torresola	
1963	John F. Kennedy	Lee Harvey Oswald	Kennedy is killed
1975	Gerald R. Ford	Lynette Fromme	Ford is unhurt
1975	Gerald R. Ford	Sara Jane Moore	Ford is unhurt
1981	Ronald Reagan	John Hinckley Jr.	Reagan is wounded

1 The diligence of special agents was crucial to the Secret Service's ability to protect President Ford from two assassination attempts in 1975. The attack by Lynette Fromme on September 5 was thwarted when Special Agent Larry Buendorf's hand pressed against her gun and prevented it from firing. (Courtesy Gerald R. Ford Library)

2 On March 31, 1981, Ronald Reagan was wounded during an assassination attempt. Fast action by his Secret Service agents saved the president's life. Six shots were fired in the assault. John Hinckley Jr. was arrested on the spot. (Courtesy Reuter's News Media, Inc./ Corbis)

COMMUNICATING THE PRESIDENCY

WITH WILLIAM L. BIRD JR.

Every president needs to use the media to communicate his values and vision to the nation. The problem is that newspapers, magazines, radio, and television are under no obligation to print or broadcast it. Originally owned by small newspaper publishers and later by large private companies, protected by the First Amendment, and imbued with a heady dose of skepticism and sometimes partisanship, the media presents every presidential administration with formidable challenges. ❡ The history of presidential-media relations is, in part, a history of struggle—between a chief executive's desire to govern and the press's commitment to the truth, between power and accountability, between authority and the people's right to know. That balance has been difficult to strike in a nation that reveres both strong presidents and the freedom of the press. ❡ In the eighteenth and nineteenth centuries presidents communicated

OPPOSITE: Franklin D. Roosevelt being filmed in the governor's Executive Mansion in Albany, New York, 1932. (Courtesy Bettmann/ Corbis)

This speaker's lectern dating to the early 1900s is believed to have been used for patriotic and community events.

through speeches, newspapers, broadsides, and handbills. The twentieth century brought new technologies that allowed presidents to communicate more effectively with more people. Radio sparked a veritable communications revolution, enabling presidents to speak directly to the masses. President Calvin Coolidge's 1925 inaugural address was carried on twenty-one radio stations to some 15 million Americans. During his first year in office "Silent Cal" spoke an average of 9,000 words per month over radio. Franklin D. Roosevelt perfected the use of the "wireless." With his rich, deep baritone and patrician inflection, Roosevelt's "fireside chats" reached across the land and into the hearts and homes of millions of Americans.

Television continued the communications revolution. The first telecast from the White House was made by Harry Truman, who was also the first president to hire a media advisor. All presidents since Truman have used television extensively, but no one has used it as adroitly as John F. Kennedy. Hollywood handsome, witty, and articulate, Kennedy sparkled before the camera, becoming America's first true television president. And what Kennedy began, Ronald Reagan finished. Reagan's use of televised addresses and carefully orchestrated media events enabled him to launch a Republican "revolution" that changed America in profound ways.

Woodrow Wilson was the first president to establish regularly scheduled press conferences, and John F. Kennedy was the first to have them televised live. But not all presidents have cared for them. For example, President Nixon, distrustful of the media, typically eschewed press conferences in favor of events over which he could exercise more control.

Today the White House is a whirlwind of public relations activity. An entire bureaucracy—including the West Wing Press Office, the Office of Media Liaison, the Office of Public Liaison, Director of Communications, speech writers, special technical advisors and others—has been created to articulate the president's views. They strive to ensure that the media reports the president in a manner that advances his political agenda.

The technology enabling the human voice to be recorded on wax cylinders allowed the president to communicate with audiences miles away.

Despite these efforts presidential control of the media has proven elusive. Committed to the people's right to know, the press has historically evinced an interest in reporting presidential misdeeds and malfeasance. No one, not even our most revered presidents, has escaped the press's zeal to report the news. Thomas Jefferson was maligned in his time for being a revolutionary and a tyrant. John Adams and John Quincy Adams were hobbled by accusations of corruption and fraud. Rutherford B. Hayes was given the moniker "His Fraudulency" for having "stolen" the 1876 election from Samuel Tilden. Even Dwight Eisenhower, the hero of World War II, suffered from embarrassing press revelations about his chief of staff, Sherman Adams. And there have been scandals galore. Ulysses S. Grant, Warren G. Harding, Richard Nixon, and William J. Clinton have all become fodder for the fourth estate.

1960 press credentials.

Hostility between the press and the media reached a high-water mark in the 1960s and 1970s, and things have never been the same. Presidential efforts to conceal information or mislead the press during the war in Vietnam and the Watergate affair, Americans' growing cynicism toward political leaders, and the burgeoning size, resources, and self-confidence of news organizations combined to transform news coverage of the presidency. Reporters began asking tougher, more probing questions. They began to look for evidence that would reveal the president as misguided at best or a liar at worst. They began to distrust the president, and the stories reflected it.

This 1977 guide reflected the increasing importance of television to presidential success.

Vietnam and Watergate rewrote the rules of political reporting. Gone was the old gentlemen's agreement, which encouraged reporters to look the other way at a president's indiscretions. Gone was the notion that presidents know best. In its place, reporters evince skepticism and cynicism. Today nothing the president says or does is sacred. Everything is second-guessed. Everything is subject to critical examination.

Reporters in the new millennium will continue to cover the president in an aggressive and uncompromising manner. In a democracy this is as it should be. And presidents, for their part, will continue their quest to use the media to advance their agenda. Chances are that whoever sits in the Oval Office in 2025 will agree with Woodrow Wilson: "Don't believe anything you read in the newspapers."

A Guide
To Your
Television Appearance

by Robert C. Diefenbach

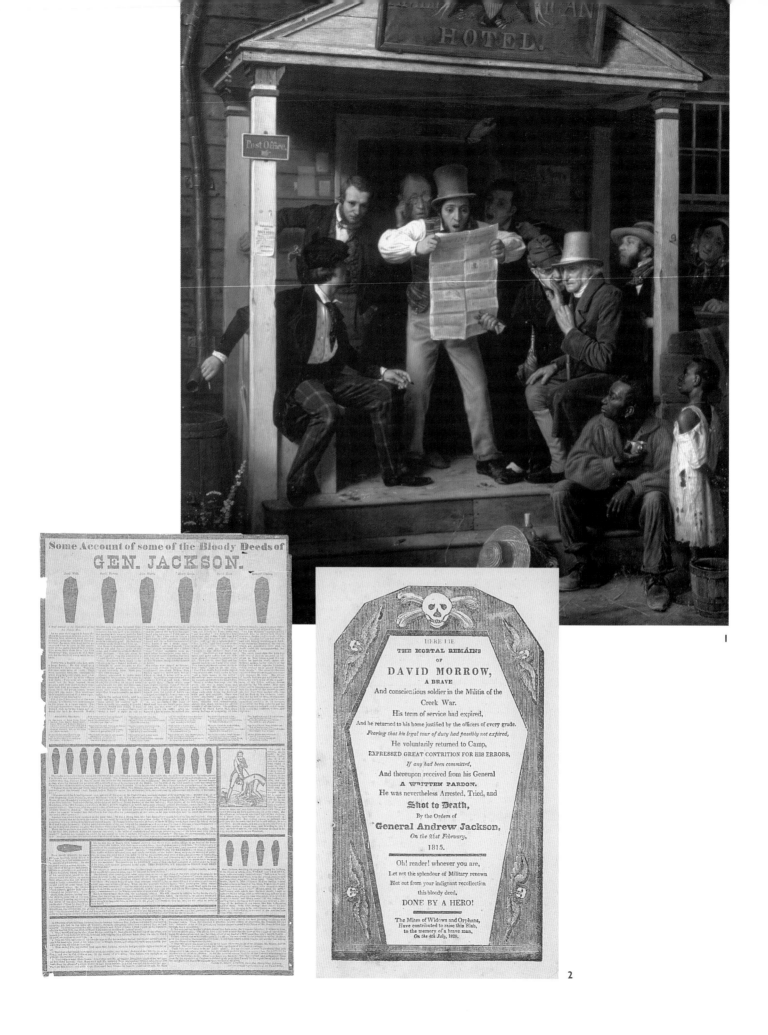

THE PRESIDENT AND THE MEDIA

The ability to communicate effectively and efficiently to the American public is one hallmark of a successful presidency. Mastering the media of the period, whether newspapers, newsreels, radio, television, or the Internet, is crucial to a president's capacity to excite people and convey the hopes and aspirations of his administration.

For some, the challenge of keeping up with the technological changes and demands in various media greatly limited their presidencies. Others achieved much politically because of their proficiency. Franklin D. Roosevelt, for instance, used the radio masterfully to speak directly to the American people, and Ronald Reagan's ease with television earned him the nickname "the Great Communicator."

SPREADING THE WORD IN PRINT

Newspapers were the dominant form of mass communication used by American presidents into the early 1900s. They disseminated ideas and projected images of a party, a candidate, and a chief executive. Along with almanacs and political biographies, they were a common means of conveying a president's message and maintaining support for the party's issues and leadership.

Political parties published their own partisan papers, a practice that began with the rivalry between Federalists and Jeffersonian Democratic–Republicans in the early 1800s. The tradition slowly faded throughout the course of the century.

I cannot, while President of the United States, descend to enter into a newspaper controversy. — Chester A. Arthur

1 Newspapers reached thousands of people, especially as literacy rates increased in the 1800s. A single copy of a newspaper served multiple readers.
↝ *War News*, 1852, by Richard Caton Woodville. (Courtesy private collection)

2 These 1828 broadsides are among the most dramatic of many printed devices that criticized the presidential ambitions and administration of Andrew Jackson. Using the striking silhouettes of coffins to represent his supposed victims, they accuse Jackson of executing militiamen under his command during the War of 1812. Despite the forceful imagery, Jackson remained powerful and popular throughout his presidency.

3 The *Log Cabin*, edited by Horace Greeley, was the leading campaign newspaper of 1840, with a circulation of 80,000. It took its title and masthead imagery from the first comprehensively merchandised symbol in American politics. The paper provided entertaining news as well as reports on the speeches and policies of soon-to-be president William Henry Harrison. Ultimately, Greeley transformed the *Log Cabin* into the *New York Tribune*.

3

1

CONNECTING WITH THE PEOPLE

Before the advent of radio, newsreels, television, or the Internet, presidents often relied on their oratorical ability to convey information and stimulate popular support. Of course, the number of people able to experience the personality and performance of the president was limited.

RECORDING THE SPOKEN WORD

2

The technology allowing the human voice to be recorded on wax cylinders became a valuable political tool in the early 1900s. The 1908 presidential race between Republican William H. Taft and Democrat William Jennings Bryan marked the first time recorded speeches were consciously used to expand the speaker's audience to those not in attendance. By 1920 presidents routinely distributed speeches and remarks on records or through transcriptions.

3

4

1 Democratic Party presidential nominee William Jennings Bryan, on the stump, addressing loggers, about 1896.
2 Wax cylinder used for recording presidential speeches in 1908.
3 Harding was the first president to deliver a speech broadcast by radio. On June 14, 1922, his talk at the dedication of the Francis Scott Key Memorial at Fort McHenry in Baltimore was broadcast by WEAR (now WFBR). Five months later a message from the president was broadcast from Washington, D.C., to twenty-eight countries.
4 Presidential candidate Harding making a phonographic recording, 1920. (Courtesy Library of Congress)
5 Capitalizing on the interest in recordings, theaters provided a setting where the public could hear candidates.
~ Theater with mannequins and recorded speeches by William Jennings Bryan, *left*, and William H. Taft, *right*.

5

HARNESSING THE AIRWAVES

By 1924, 1.25 million American households had a radio, compared to 400,000 the previous year. By the early 1930s the two largest networks, the National Broadcasting Company and the Columbia Broadcasting System, were quickly becoming national fixtures. Ubiquitous and immediate, radio was now the foremost medium of mass communication, and the radio receiver was a primary focus in the American home.

62,100,000
61,365,000
50,100,000
79.0
78.1
57.0
Dec. 11, 1941
message to people DEC. 9, 1941
Three high purposes FEB. 23, 1942

6,300,000
13,700,000
10,900,000
16,400,000
15,000,000
19,100,000
10,300,000
9.7
23.1
16.2
23.5
22.9
27.5
15.4
21.
31.4
Stab-in-the-back JUNE
Arsenal of democracy
OCT. 12, 1940
1936
OCT. 10, 1936
OCT. 21, 1936
JAN. 8, 1936
NOV. 4, 1938
JAN. 8, 1940
MAY 3, 1940

3

4

5

1 Presidents Coolidge and Hoover occasionally were heard on the radio, but they did not understand the potential impact of the new medium. ∼ President Hoover delivering the final address of the 1932 campaign from his private railroad car. (Courtesy Herbert Hoover Library)

2 Franklin D. Roosevelt, a master of timing and tone, was the first president to effectively use radio. In the inimitable style of his "fireside chats," he voiced his beliefs and programs directly to the American people. In return, his audience believed Roosevelt was responsible for their personal well-being and improvement. ∼ NBC microphone used by Roosevelt.

3 The radio became a major source of news during the 1930s. Here two Farm Security Administration clients are posed in their Hidalgo County, Texas, home to show the centrality of radio in their lives, 1939. (Courtesy Bettmann/ Corbis)

4 Broadcast industry executives were especially interested in quantifying radio listening. This chart, prepared by the Hooper Ratings Company, illustrates the steady growth of the listening audience for Roosevelt's radio addresses from 1936 to 1942. (Courtesy Franklin D. Roosevelt Library)

5 During the 1930s and 1940s this cathedral-style radio became a fixture in many American homes. Presidents and political leaders soon tailored their speaking style to appeal to this growing audience.

THE PRESIDENTIAL SCREEN

Motion picture newsreels were an important means of mass communication from the 1920s through the late 1940s. By the 1930s some 85 million Americans attended one of 17,000 movie theaters each week. At most film screenings these moviegoers saw newsreels—short subjects, updated twice a week—from five companies: Fox Movietone, News of the Day, Paramount, RKO-Pathé, and Universal.

The newsreel helped the film industry cement political connections with Washington. And it gave many Americans their first look at the "performance" of presidential speeches and addresses, projecting personality in a way that would become increasingly familiar through radio and television in the coming years.

THE BROADCAST IMAGE

By the 1950s presidents realized that much of their time and much of their money should be spent on television. Franklin D. Roosevelt had been the first president seen on television, in 1939. A more important event occurred in 1952, however, when Dwight Eisenhower became the first presidential candidate to appear in a television campaign commercial. His unorthodox decision surprised many, but the power of television was soon apparent, and President Eisenhower used the medium to his advantage through both of his terms in office.

Since the 1952 election television has been the dominant medium for the expression of presidential leadership. In today's political environment, manufacturing an effective presidential image requires the use of newspapers and news magazines, talk radio, television, and ever increasingly, the Internet.

> The media are far more powerful than the president in creating public awareness and shaping public opinion, for the simple reason that the media always have the last word.   Richard M. Nixon

1 This Akeley newsreel camera belonged to Joseph W. Gibson, a cameraman whose career started in 1914 at New Jersey's Fort Lee Studios. He subsequently worked for five news organizations and used the camera from 1935 to 1959.

2 The Trans-Lux Theater on Broadway in Manhattan, shown here in 1931, presented a changing program of newsreels lasting about forty-five minutes.

3 Motion picture and still photographers on the White House lawn, 1919. (Courtesy Library of Congress)

Sept. 29, 1952.

Dear friend,
This is just a note to
tell you how deeply Pat
and I appreciated your
expression of confidence
after the broadcast last
Tuesday.
We want you to know
we shall do our best
never to let you down.
Dick Nixon

U. S. POSTAGE
2c PAID
Washington, D. C.
Permit 6149

458

4 Richard Nixon's televised "Checkers speech" demonstrated that diligent preparation and mastery of production details could position a candidate in a favorable light. The speech was a response to allegations in the press that Nixon had used campaign funds for personal expenses. The charge jeopardized his place on the 1952 Republican Party ticket. The broadcast's most memorable feature was Nixon's account of how his children received Checkers, a black-and-white cocker spaniel, from "a man down in Texas who heard Pat on the radio mention the fact that our two youngsters would like to have a dog."

The dramatic quality of Nixon's speech, his heartfelt delivery, and his insistence that the family would keep Checkers "no matter what" struck a chord among viewers. A stream of sympathetic cards and supportive letters flooded the campaign. Relieved staffers responded to each one with a picture postcard of the vice-presidential candidate and his family.

Newsweek

THE **TV DEBATES**
AND **STORMY K**

How Much Influence
on the Election?
[50-STATE LISTENING POST SURVEY]

25c
OCTOBER 10, 1960
[INDEX—PAGE 15]

Pila

1

2

3

4

1 John F. Kennedy accepting the presidential nomination at the Los Angeles Democratic National Convention, July 15, 1960. (Courtesy Bettmann/Corbis)

2 *Newsweek* and other picture magazines continued to play an important role into the early 1970s when their visual and reportorial functions were eclipsed by television. This 1960 issue helped thousands of Americans to better understand the importance of the Nixon–Kennedy debates.

3 Kennedy was the first president to allow live television broadcast of his press conferences. (Courtesy John F. Kennedy Library)

4 Walter Cronkite covering the 1968 Democratic National Convention. (Courtesy CBS)

5 To monitor the nightly newscasts of the three major networks—NBC, CBS, and ABC—Lyndon Johnson had a special console of three televisions installed in the Oval Office. (Courtesy Lyndon Baines Johnson Library)

5

I can think of nothing more boring, for the American public, than to have to sit in their living rooms for a whole half an hour looking at my face on their television screens.

Dwight D. Eisenhower

THE INTERNET

Bill Clinton was the first president with the opportunity to make effective use of the Internet. Like the rest of us, those in the White House are exploring and expanding the use of digital media to reach growing audiences. The ability to communicate directly to millions of Americans without having to rely on the traditional media to carry the message is already changing how the president addresses the nation and how citizens can respond. We are only just now seeing how great a change this might make.

4

5

1 *Meet the Press,* the longest-running series on television, debuted on November 6, 1947. Conceived as a radio program to promote publisher Lawrence E. Spivak's *American Mercury* magazine, *Meet the Press* brought televised political discussions into American living rooms. In its earliest guise the program's half-hour format featured Spivak, *left,* as moderator and sometime panelist, a panel of four Washington journalists, and a guest. Today the show is more of a conversation than an unrehearsed press conference. (Courtesy Library of Congress)
~ The moderator's desk and chair and the signage date to 1975, the year Spivak retired from the program.
2 TelePrompTer text read by Vice President Walter F. Mondale at the 1984 Democratic National Convention.
3 Leaving little to chance, today's nominat-

ing conventions are meticulously produced television events. This light cluster functioned as the "go light" used by Republican National Convention managers in 1996 to pace and—when needed—prod the speakers.

Attached to the lectern out of public sight, yet in plain view of the speaker, the green light signaled that all was well; yellow cautioned to quickly wrap up; red meant running long. According to technicians working behind the scenes, yellow and red signals were seldom given, as most speakers stuck to the script, reading their carefully prepared and paced remarks from a TelePrompTer.
4 Bill Clinton in the White House (Courtesy White House)
5 Jimmy Carter giving an address to the nation from the Oval Office, 1977. (Courtesy Jimmy Carter Library)

THE PRESIDENCY IN POPULAR IMAGINATION

More than wielders of power, presidents are deeply symbolic, even iconic, figures who have played a dominant role in shaping and reflecting American culture. Whether as emblems of democracy or as the embodiment of everything that is great, good, or evil in America, presidents, from the beginning of the Republic until today, have carved out a permanent place in popular imagination. ❡ Their influence is everywhere. We name cities, towns, streets, bridges, and schools after presidents. We ape their fashion sense: men stopped wearing hats in 1961 because JFK never wore one. We put their likenesses on money and on postage stamps. We visit Mount Rushmore, the Washington Monument, and the Jefferson Memorial. We make pilgrimages to Mount Vernon, Montpelier, Monticello, and other presidential homes to gaze at the fine eighteenth-century chairs and tables, and to marvel at

OPPOSITE: Ad for Cherry Smash Soda, ca. 1916–1919.

This peanut bank acknowledges Jimmy Carter's background as a peanut farmer as well as his toothy smile.

All presidents are not remembered equally. James
Polk and Ulysses Grant
were once quite popular,
yet few Americans now
visit the once marred
Grant's Tomb in New
York City and fewer
Americans still know
Polk's name or accom-
plishments. Other presi-
dents became icons,
whose memory is en-
shrined in monuments
or historic sites: *top*, Lincoln Memorial (Cour-
tesy Harry S. Truman
Library); *left*, Monticello
(Courtesy Thomas Jef-
ferson Memorial Foun-
dation, Inc.); *right*,
Mount Vernon (Cour-
tesy Mount Vernon
Ladies' Association).

THE EXCITING NEW GAME OF
THE **KENNEDYS**

The popularity of John F. Kennedy led to the creation of this board game in 1962.

Thomas Jefferson's uncanny inventions. But we also go to see, touch, and pay homage to these larger-than-life figures who pervade our popular culture. The presidents inhabit our collective memory in part because of an astonishing array of media. Portraits, photographs, film, television, folk songs, Broadway musicals, advertisements, and souvenirs have all served to celebrate, criticize, satirize, sell, legitimize, exploit, praise, and memorialize the holders of this office.

GEORGE BUSH DR

Street sign with presidential name. (Lent by the Traffic Department, College Station, Texas)

These popular culture sources of memory may help explain why we tend to confuse presidential fact and fiction. For example, the famous tale of George Washington and the cherry tree was invented by the preacher and author Mason Locke Weems (1759–1825), who added the tale to the fifth edition of his book, *The Life and Memorable Actions of George Washington* (c. 1800). Likewise, many Americans' knowledge of presidents such as Abraham Lincoln is shaped more by cinematic depictions by Henry Fonda and Raymond Massey than the works of hundreds of historians. More recently, millions of Americans see the White House through the prism of weekly television shows such as *The West Wing*.

The image of the president does not ensure the quality or propriety of a souvenir. The plastic case, *above left*, contains one pencil for each president. The whistle, *below*, recalls Theodore Roosevelt's buckteeth, one of his more prominent and caricatured features.

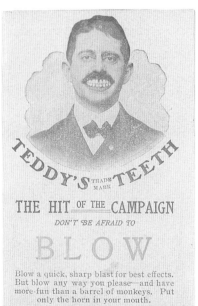

TEDDY'S TRADE MARK TEETH

THE HIT OF THE CAMPAIGN

DON'T BE AFRAID TO

BLOW

Blow a quick, sharp blast for best effects. But blow any way you please—and have more fun than a barrel of monkeys. Put only the horn in your mouth.

As a symbol of and for America, the president was traditionally depicted as a heroic figure, as the nation's moral compass, or as a reflection of the national mood. Changing technologies and changing attitudes have contributed to a more accessible and more varied depiction of the president, thought not a necessarily more realistic one. The centrality and visibility of the presidency in American culture speaks volumes about the importance and influence of the president and contributes to the creation of a common political culture.

BORN TO COMMAND.

OF VETO MEMORY.

CONSTITUTION
of the
UNITED STATES
of America.

KING ANDREW THE FIRST.

THE CARTOONING OF THE PRESIDENCY

Using drawings or cartoons to comment on the actions of a president is a tradition nearly as old as the nation. Cartoons help make complex issues and personalities more accessible to a wide public. They often have a great effect on attitudes about a chief executive. Many presidents felt like William "Boss" Tweed, a nineteenth-century New York politician who bemoaned the influence of negative cartoons: "Stop them damn pictures. . . . I don't care much about what the papers write about me. My constituents can't read. But, damn it, they can see pictures."

The pen is mightier than the politician.

Gerald R. Ford

Political cartoons were the creation of the partisan press supporting either the Federalists or the Jeffersonian Republicans in the early 1800s. They became staples of weekly magazines during the nineteenth century and eventually became a cornerstone of the modern newspaper industry.

1 President Jackson pursued his agenda forcefully. Many political opponents, fearing Jackson's use of power, called him "King Andrew."

This 1832 cartoon shows Jackson trampling on the Constitution. The cartoon garnered support for the opposing Whig Party, but it did little to thwart Jackson's desire to increase the power of the presidency. (Courtesy Library of Congress)

2 The presidency of Teddy Roosevelt reinvigorated the arena of political satire. Roosevelt's features, especially his wide mouth and constant movement while speaking, were a cartoonist's delight.

~ Early twentieth-century cartoon by Gustav Brandt captures the essence of Teddy Roosevelt.

3 Called "Silent Cal" by the press, Calvin Coolidge was a frugal and prim New Englander who was often satirized by cartoonists. In this 1929 *Life* cartoon by Gluyas Williams, Coolidge's image is parodied when a lost boot threatens to prevent him from leaving the White House at the end of his term.

4 Richard Nixon was elected president in 1968 in a campaign that promised to return "law and order" to the country. Yet he used wiretapping to spy on many Americans he felt were opposed to his policies. This 1974 cartoon by Tim Mitelberg suggests that Nixon's actions were breaking the very laws he promised to uphold. Nixon was forced out of office in 1974, in part because of the content of tapes he made of conversations in the White House. (Courtesy Cartoonist & Writer Syndicate)

3

4

THE PRESIDENCY IN MOVIES AND TELEVISION

The presidency has always been an element of feature films, although movies depicting actual or fictional presidents have rarely been box-office successes. Early silent classics included *Lincoln, the Lover* (1914) and *The Birth of a Nation* (1915).

Some films sought to glorify *(Young Mr. Lincoln, Sunrise at Campobello, PT 109)*; others explored the ambiguity of the office *(Seven Days in May, Nixon, Dr. Strangelove)*. More recent movies, like *Air Force One, Deep Impact,* and *The American President,* turned the president into an action hero, a romantic leading man, or a symbol of all that is good—or wrong—in America.

Television has treated the executive office in a less reverential manner. In the early years programs like *Producer's Showcase* and *Philco Playhouse* began to examine the American political system. By the 1970s several depictions of the presidency attempted to demystify and to explain, including *Eleanor and Franklin, Collision Course,* and *The Missiles of October.*

NBC's *The West Wing* tried to both entertain and educate its viewers about life in a working White House while *Saturday Night Live, The Daily Show with Jon Stewart,* and all the late night talk shows satirize the presidency on a regular basis.

1 The majority of American presidents have been ignored by the film industry. The 1944 movie *Wilson,* with Alexander Knox, is one of the few that explores the life and administration of Woodrow Wilson, president from 1913 to 1921.

2 The wartime exploits of John F. Kennedy are heroically chronicled in *PT 109,* a 1963 movie starring Cliff Robertson. Its popularity was tied in part to the nation's reaction to the assassination of President Kennedy on November 22, 1963.

3 The 1964 Warner Brothers feature *Kisses for My President* stars Polly Bergen as the first woman to serve as president and Fred MacMurray as her husband. Bergen is so overwhelmed by the strains of the job that when she discovers she is pregnant, she happily resigns. The film clearly reflects many of the attitudes that shaped women's lives in the early 1960s.

4 *Dr. Strangelove* was directed by Stanley Kubrick and has a strong ensemble cast led by Peter Sellers. Called the "first nuclear comedy," this 1964 film is important because it breaks the mold of depicting the American president in a heroic manner. Here, the president is rife with indecision.

5 *The Man,* made in 1972, features James Earl Jones as the nation's first black president. He successfully battles race, politics, and presidential crises.

6 Recent examinations of the presidency, such as the 1994 Nick Nolte vehicle, *Jefferson in Paris,* attempt to move beyond a heroic examination of the past. This feature depicts the third president as a brilliant but flawed individual, a very different interpretation of Thomas Jefferson than that of earlier films.

7 Poster showcasing *Air Force One,* a 1997 movie with Harrison Ford as a heroic chief executive who defeats terrorists highjacking the presidential airplane.

2

3

4

5

6

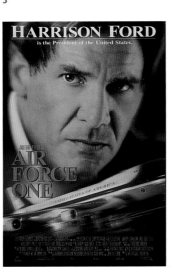

7

On September 22, 1999, *The West Wing*, a series exploring the lives of those who work in the White House, debuted on NBC. Produced by Aaron Sorkin, *The West Wing* became one of the most popular shows on television. Objects used in making the series include this script, prop campaign button, and windbreaker worn by Martin Sheen, who plays the president. (Courtesy Aaron Sorkin)

THE PRESIDENCY IN SONG

The presidency has been memorialized in nearly every genre of American song. Campaign ditties are written to captivate the voters, blues recordings express racial frustrations and hopes, and Broadway musicals often provide a lighthearted treatment.

An astonishing number of America's premier performers and songwriters have explored the subject. They include Leonard Bernstein, George and Ira Gershwin, Jackie "Moms" Mabley, Frank Sinatra, Johnny Horton, John Philip Sousa, and Irving Berlin. Few of the songs are memorable, but they demonstrate the importance and the visibility of the president.

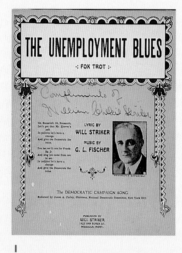

1 Since the early nineteenth century, presidential candidates have used campaign songs to attract voters' attention. One of the more unusual songs, "The Unemployment Blues," was used by candidate Franklin D. Roosevelt to suggest that the average working man was devastated by the economic policies of President Herbert Hoover.

2 The tradition of lampooning the president extends back to Mark Twain and Will Rogers. Record albums like *The First Family,* produced in 1962 and featuring Vaughn Meader, spoofed President Kennedy's unmistakable New England accent.

3 Written by Dick Holler in reaction to the assassinations of Kennedy and Martin Luther King Jr., the song "Abraham, Martin, and John," captured the country's shock and grief in a manner that made it a constant presence on the airwaves in 1968 and 1969. The song was recorded by Dion, Smokey Robinson and the Miracles, and Jackie "Moms" Mabley.

4 Presidents have often been the subject of Broadway productions. In the 1970s and 1980s small ensembles and one-person plays brought the personalities of presidents like Abraham Lincoln and Lyndon Johnson to the stage. James Whitmore's stellar performance as Harry Truman is captured in this 1975 recording of *Give 'Em Hell, Harry!*

TO MOVE THE BOWELS

TAKE LINCOLN TEA

AN HONEST MAN

AN HONEST MEDICINE

"IT WORKS WITHOUT A GRIPE"

"TAKE A DOSE TO NIGHT."

25 CENT PACKAGE

LINCOLN TEA

THE BEST BLOOD PURIFIER

FOR SALE AT DRUG STORES.

5

OF INTEREST TO TRAVELERS
IN THE UNITED STATES AND ABROAD

ROOSEVELT went to SOUTH AMERICA

A·B·A Certified Cheques

...appreciate ...venience ...eques for ...re Roose... ...s South ...in 1913-... ...Certified ...you, too, these official travelers cheques of the American Bankers Association. A·B·A Cheques are recognized and accepted at favorable

rates in banks, hotels, shops and ticket offices in all parts of the world. They are better than gold because they afford complete protection against loss or theft. U. S. Government customs officials accept them at all ports. A·B·A Cheques are the only certified travel cheques that enjoy universal acceptance. Yet they cost no more than ordinary travel funds. 11,000 banks advise their use. Get them from your bank.

This Book Free
Whenever any A·B·A Cheques for use abroad your bank will give you a copy of Harry Franck's "All About Going Abroad," a Brentano book sold in bookstores at $1.00.

Better Than Gold

A·B·A Certified CHEQUES

This cheque is certified by BANKERS TRUST COMPANY, NEW YORK, Agent for the issuing bank, and is the only authorized travel cheque of the American Bankers Association.

In writing to advertisers

6

Jefferson Towers

5 This ad for Lincoln Tea attempted to draw a parallel between Lincoln, "an honest man," and Lincoln Tea, "an honest medicine." The name and image of Lincoln evokes ideals of integrity and goodness—values that the manufacturer hoped to impart on its product.
6 In the early twentieth century the image of Theodore Roosevelt was very popular among advertisers. His vigor, enthusiastic personality, and credibility as both president and war hero lent legitimacy to any product. Here Roosevelt's reputation as an international adventurer is used to sell American Bankers Association Travelers Cheques.

CONSUMING THE OFFICE: PRESIDENTIAL IMAGES IN ADVERTISING

Presidential images have been used by advertisers since the nineteenth century to encourage people to buy products and services. The chief executive is a symbol of progress, optimism, and personal achievement—valuable characteristics that influence consumers.

Having the president's image in an ad—especially that of Washington, Jefferson, or Theodore Roosevelt—helped legitimize a product and separate it from the competition. His name or representation instantly made an item recognizable and in demand. In the twentieth century an unwritten rule mandates against using the image of the current president to advertise goods.

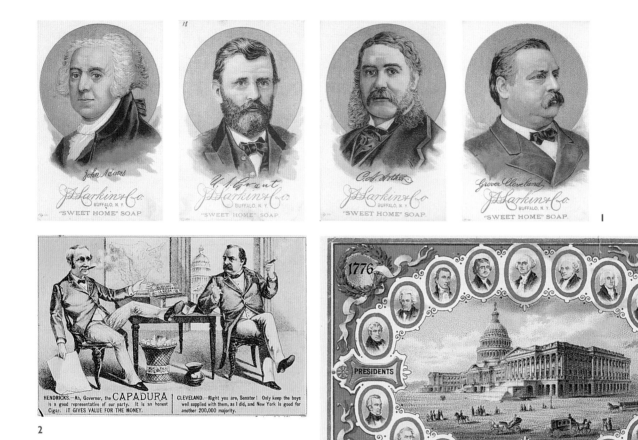

John Adams
JD Larkin & Co
BUFFALO, N.Y.
"SWEET HOME" SOAP.

U. S. Grant
JD Larkin & Co
BUFFALO, N.Y.
"SWEET HOME" SOAP.

Ch. Arthur
JD Larkin & Co
BUFFALO, N.Y.
"SWEET HOME" SOAP.

Grover Cleveland,
JD Larkin & Co
BUFFALO, N.Y.
"SWEET HOME" SOAP.

1

HENDRICKS.—Ah, Governor, the **CAPADURA** is a good representative of our party. It is an honest Cigar. IT GIVES VALUE FOR THE MONEY.

CLEVELAND.—Right you are, Senator! Only keep the boys well supplied with them, as I did, and New York is good for another 200,000 majority.

2

1776 — 1876

PRESIDENTS

UNITED STATES

1876 — 1776

3

1 Companies used presidential images like John Adams, Ulysses Grant, Chester Arthur, and Grover Cleveland—here gracing advertising cards for Sweet Home Soap—to encourage sales of their product. Trade cards were created by wholesalers so that retailers could give customers an attractive reminder of what products to purchase. In use primarily from the years just after the Civil War through the early twentieth century, trade cards allowed people to collect a bit of the presidency for themselves. **2** This ad associates the "honesty" and "value" of Capadura-brand cigars with President Cleveland and the Democratic party. **3** This postcard advertisement uses images of the presidents to sell clothing for the E. Bingham & Sons Company, ca. 1876. **4** As America celebrated its centennial in 1876, companies created games, like this one from the McLoughlin Brothers, to encourage children to learn the history of the presidency. **5** The California citrus industry began to market its products throughout the nation in the early twentieth century, thanks in part to quicker and more reliable transportation. Many of the shipping and advertising labels for oranges and lemons depicted idealized images of California. But the Victoria Avenue Citrus Association opted to use the image of Lincoln to evoke feelings of familiarity, pride, and nationalism. **6** Not always humorous or benign, souvenirs can provide an opportunity to criticize the president or his policies. This 1967 dart game reflects opposition to Lyndon Johnson's decision to escalate the war in Vietnam.

4

1776 — 1876
CENTENNIAL PRESIDENTIAL GAME
McLOUGHLIN BROS.

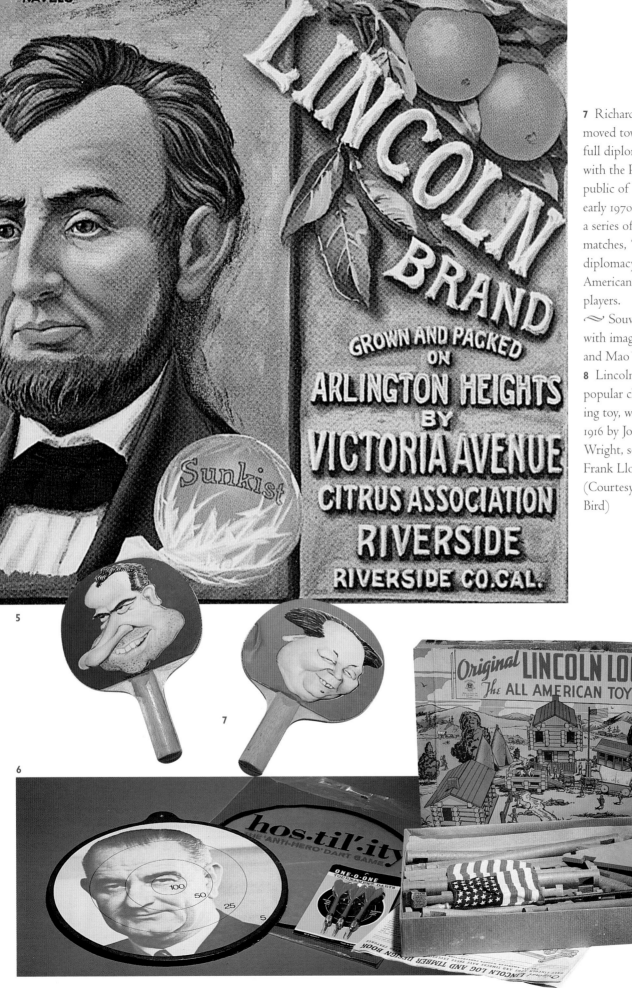

7 Richard Nixon slowly moved toward opening full diplomatic relations with the People's Republic of China. In the early 1970s, he arranged a series of table tennis matches, "Ping-Pong diplomacy," between American and Chinese players.

〜 Souvenir paddles, with images of Nixon and Mao Tse-tung.

8 Lincoln Logs, the popular children's building toy, was invented in 1916 by John Lloyd Wright, son of architect Frank Lloyd Wright. (Courtesy William L. Bird)

CAPTURING AN ESSENCE: THE PRESIDENCY AS A SOUVENIR

Collecting souvenirs is a centuries-old phenomenon that evolved from religious pilgrimages and migrations of communities. It sustains memories and captures the essence of a journey, event, place, or individual.

Maintaining a memory of the presidency through a keepsake allows people to honor or own a piece of the presidential past. Souvenirs range from relics to expensive and unique items to cheaper, mass-produced toys, T-shirts, and mugs— "star-spangled kitsch." Except for iconic items most of this material is quickly forgotten or discarded by the purchaser or recipient. But it reveals much about changing notions of how a president can or should be remembered.

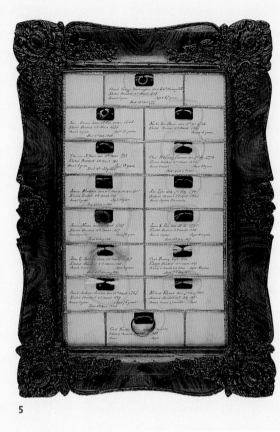

5

6

7

8

1 During the 1932 bicentennial of George Washington's birth, plays and pageants performed in costumes like this one were presented throughout the nation.

2 Souvenirs bearing the image of Andrew Jackson flourished during and after "Old Hickory's" presidency. This souvenir snuffbox, about 1828, depicts Jackson as a military hero.

3 Glass paperweights have been popular souvenirs since the 1860s. This twentieth-century paperweight bears the

image of President McKinley.

4 This cardboard sewing box, from about 1824, has an image of John Quincy Adams on the inside lid.

5 Today the idea of collecting hair may seem morbid or bizarre but in the eighteenth and nineteenth centuries, it was an acceptable way to mourn and remember the dead. This display, which came to the Smithsonian in 1883, contains hair from presidents Washington, John Adams, Jefferson, Madi-

son, Monroe, John Quincy Adams, Jackson, Van Buren, Harrison, Tyler, Polk, Taylor, Fillmore, and Pierce.

6 Twentieth-century glass paperweight with the likeness of President Jefferson.

7 This 1831 comb, a token of appreciation, features Jackson's image surrounded by those of Washington and the Marquis de Lafayette.

8 This doll depicts Theodore Roosevelt in his Rough Rider uniform from the 1898 Spanish-American War.

LIFE AFTER THE PRESIDENCY

Finally, after four years—eight, if favored with reelection—the president must bid farewell to the White House. For him there will be no more cabinet meetings, press conferences, or state dinners. It is time to leave Washington, time to enter the annals of history. ❧ Some presidents are reluctant to go. There are so many unfinished plans, so many dreams deferred. Others have left and never looked back. When former president Calvin Coolidge filled out a membership form for the Washington Press Club, he wrote "retired," and the aside, "And glad of it." ❧ Whether they savored the limelight or simply tolerated the burdens of office, each president has had to face the question, what comes next? ❧ The Constitution offers no answer. It states how long the president's term shall be but not what the nation should do with or for former presidents. Consequently, the lives of our retired presidents

OPPOSITE: President Reagan leaves Washington in Marine One after President George Bush's inauguration. (Courtesy Ronald Reagan Library)

The Grants received this Coptic Bible in Gibraltar while on a two-year world tour after leaving office.

British sovereign given to the United States by James Smithson. Congressman John Quincy Adams—after his years as president—championed the cause of Smithson's unusual bequest, leading to the establishment of the Smithsonian Institution in 1846.

have varied. Some, like Harry Truman, have gone home to lead quiet lives. Others have chosen to stay active in public life. John Quincy Adams and Andrew Johnson returned to Washington as members of Congress, and in 1861 John Tyler died a member of the Confederate House of Representatives. Similarly, in 1921 former president William H. Taft was appointed chief justice of the Supreme Court, a position he considered his greatest honor: "I don't remember that I ever was president," he quipped. More recently, President Carter returned to Georgia, where in 1982 he founded the nonprofit Carter Center in Atlanta to promote peace and human rights worldwide.

Although George Washington and John Adams could simply retire to their farms, it has proven difficult for modern ex-presidents to re-capture their older, simpler lives. When Coolidge retired and tried to travel with his wife, Grace, they were met by tremendous crowds that severely restricted their ability to visit places of interest. Their ex-periences foreshadowed the need for protection and compensation that later presidents would receive. Beginning with legislation passed in 1958, Congress gave former chief executives an annual salary of $25,000, free office space, free mailing privileges, $25,000 for clerical assistance, and a $10,000-a-year pension to the widows of former presidents. Ten years later Secret Service protection for life—or until the widow remarried—was added.

America has recognized the wisdom of providing former presidents with benefits, but we have yet to recognize—and capitalize on—the value of their wisdom and expertise. These are men who have spent years studying and analyzing the economy, military challenges, foreign policy questions, and a host of other issues critical to the nation. Shouldn't we put them to better use?

Different thoughts on that subject have been offered over the years. One idea set forth by William Jennings Bryan was that all former presidents become ex-officio members of the Senate. In 1916 Congressman J. Hampton Moore sponsored legislation to create a permanent House seat for former presidents that would pay a salary of $25,000 a year. Similar legislation to make former presidents honorary or sitting members of the Senate or House has been offered on a regular basis since 1944. None has passed.

Sitting presidents have typically been reluctant to tap the ad-

Souvenir program from dinner honoring Theodore Roosevelt after his return from a Smithsonian-sponsored African expedition, 1909-1910.

George Bush with Mikhail Gorbachev and Margaret Thatcher, October 1995. (Courtesy George Bush Library)

advice of former presidents, particularly when the two hail from different parties or adhere to different political points of view. Given their very different outlook on the role of the federal government, Thomas Jefferson was probably pleased when John Adams quit Washington and retired to his farm. Warren G. Harding and Ronald Reagan were, likewise, keen to distance themselves from their respective predecessors, Woodrow Wilson and Jimmy Carter.

Even when their ideas match, sitting presidents generally prefer to demonstrate independence from their predecessors. One need only look at the presidencies of Ulysses S. Grant and Rutherford B. Hayes, or of Richard Nixon and Gerald Ford to understand how important it was for Hayes and Ford to establish identities that were distinct from their predecessors'.

Numbers may also explain why we have failed to address the question of what to do with our ex-presidents. Historically, it has been unusual to have more than two living ex-presidents at any one time. The standing record for many years dates to the 1860s, when Van Buren, Tyler, Fillmore, Pierce, and Buchanan were alive during Abraham Lincoln's administration. This record was only recently matched. When Bill Clinton was inaugurated in 1993 there were five living former presidents—Nixon, Ford, Carter, Reagan, and Bush. That number may grow yet, with the increasing longevity of the American population and the constitutional limitation of just two terms for any future president.

Hillary, Bill, and Chelsea Clinton at Martha's Vineyard. (Courtesy Folio, Inc.)

AFTER THE WHITE HOUSE WHAT DO PRESIDENTS DO?

There is no prescribed role for presidents after leaving office. Their activities often depend on their standing in the eyes of the American people, stature within their party, or desire to continue in the public realm.

The retiring president does not want his prestige used in a manner he feels is inappropriate, nor does the incumbent want to be upstaged by the previous officeholder. Each former chief executive must approach the challenge in his own way. There are no right answers, only individual attempts to find a level of contentment after having held the most powerful job in the nation.

Well, there doesn't seem to be anything else for an ex-president to do but go into the country and raise big pumpkins. Chester A. Arthur

GEORGE WASHINGTON RETURNS HOME

George Washington set the pattern for many presidents when he chose a quiet retirement at his beloved Mount Vernon. There he spent time with his family, surveying the land and tending to much-needed repairs on the property. Upon retiring Washington confessed, "I shall resign the chair of government without a single regret." He died at age 67, nine months before his successor, John Adams, moved into the White House.

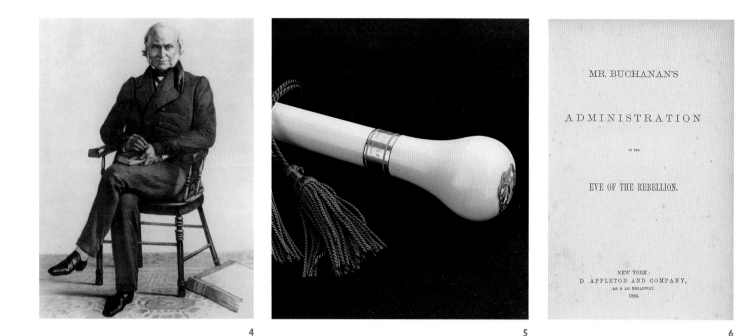

4

5

6

1 Washington, in a watercolor by Benjamin Henry Latrobe, using a telescope at Mount Vernon, Virginia. (Courtesy Mount Vernon Ladies' Association)

2 George Washington's telescope.

3 This chair was located near Washington's bed. It is thought he sat in it not long before he died.

4 John Quincy Adams, 1843. (Courtesy Library of Congress)

5 Adams received this ivory cane from Julius Pratt & Company of Meriden, Connecticut. It was given to him for his efforts to end the gag rule, which prevented discussions in the House of Representatives about the abolition of slavery.

6 In 1866 Buchanan wrote the first published presidential memoir, *Mr. Buchanan's Administration on the Eve of the Rebellion*, in part to justify his leadership and place in history.

JOHN QUINCY ADAMS REMAINS A PUBLIC SERVANT

A year after leaving office, John Quincy Adams won election to the U.S. House of Representatives from Massachusetts. During his seventeen years as a congressman he actively supported the anti-slavery movement and promoted the establishment of the Smithsonian Institution. Adams was the only former president to serve in the House, and Andrew Johnson was the only one to serve in the Senate.

JAMES BUCHANAN DEFENDS HIS PRESIDENCY

James Buchanan became president in 1857 with a distinguished record in political life. He left in 1861, scorned by friends and foes alike. His fall from grace was promoted by the growing crisis between the North and South. The Dred Scott decision, the outbreak of violence between pro- and anti-slavery supporters in Kansas, and abolitionist John Brown's 1859 raid on a federal arsenal in Harper's Ferry, Virginia, occurred during his presidency, inflamed sectional feeling, and severely tested his leadership and vision. Unable to provide innovative leadership, Buchanan served the remainder of his term, and retired to his Pennsylvania mansion, Wheatland, in 1861, where he wrote a memoir that recounted his troubled presidency.

ULYSSES S. GRANT DISTANCES HIMSELF FROM OFFICE

Ulysses and Julia Grant, accompanied by their son Jesse, traveled extensively throughout Asia, Europe, and Africa after the inauguration of Rutherford B. Hayes. During the last years of his administration, charges of corruption coupled with the worst economic depression yet experienced by the nation damaged Grant's popularity and encouraged this grand tour. During their trip the Grants were greeted and honored with gifts by local dignitaries, including Pope Leo XIII. Their travels in the late 1870s lasted more than two years and soon were followed by visits to Cuba, the West Indies, and Mexico.

THEODORE ROOSEVELT REMAINS "VIGOROUS"

Noted for his advocacy of the "vigorous life," Teddy Roosevelt did not retire quietly. He traveled to Africa in 1909–10 with naturalists and taxidermists from the Smithsonian to acquire specimens. He then toured Europe, returning to the United States as popular as ever.

Unhappy with the administration of his successor, William Howard Taft, Roosevelt eventually formed an alternative Progressive Party. He did not win the national election of 1912, but remained visible, writing books, traveling to Brazil, editing magazines, and campaigning for the Republican presidential nominee in 1916.

4 WILLIAM HOWARD TAFT SERVES THE COUNTRY—AGAIN

Yale University appointed William Howard Taft the Kent professor of law after he retired. Later, he lectured and wrote articles for national magazines. In 1920 Taft actively supported Warren G. Harding's bid for the presidency. One year later Harding appointed Taft chief justice of the Supreme Court. Taft is the only president to serve as chief justice. He held this position, and that of chancellor of the Smithsonian Institution, for the next ten years.

5

6

7

1

2

3

DWIGHT D. EISENHOWER ENJOYS HIS LEISURE

Immensely popular as president, Dwight D. Eisenhower retired to his farm in Gettysburg, Pennsylvania, after leaving office. Many claim he would have been elected a third time, if not for the Twenty-Second Amendment to the Constitution barring more than two terms as president. Eisenhower wrote his memoirs, supported the Vietnam War, and endorsed Richard Nixon's 1968 bid for the Republican presidential nomination. Golf was his passion, and scoring a hole in one in 1968 was an accomplishment that gave him great delight.

LYNDON JOHNSON RETURNS TO TEXAS

Following the inauguration of Richard Nixon on January 20, 1969, Lyndon Johnson returned to Texas, where his political career had begun nearly forty years before. He wrote his memoirs, *The Vantage Point*, taught students, and attended the dedication of the Lyndon Baines Johnson Library. Johnson played a key role in organizing the library's first symposium, which brought together scholars and leaders in the field of education. The former president also helped to organize a national symposium on civil rights, a major concern of his administration.

4

5

RICHARD NIXON— REHABILITATING AN IMAGE

Accused of abusing presidential power for his role in the coverup of the Watergate scandal, Richard Nixon resigned from the presidency on August 8, 1974—the first and only president to resign from office. He was pardoned by his successor, Gerald Ford, and spent the remaining twenty years of his life in the public eye, working tirelessly to rescue his reputation. In books, on radio, and in television interviews, Nixon reminded Americans of one of his administration's greatest achievements: the opening of diplomatic relations between the United States and China. By the time of his death in 1994, Nixon, for some Americans, had achieved the status of an elder statesman.

JIMMY CARTER AND WORLD PEACE

After leaving office in 1981, President Carter established the Carter Center, a non-partisan institute that addresses national and international issues of public policy. The Center, built in conjunction with the Carter Library and Museum at Emory University in Atlanta, has brought together a variety of political leaders, scholars, and others to resolve conflict, promote democracy, and protect human rights. Since his presidency, Carter has published numerous books, and remains a highly visible proponent of world peace.

1 Dwight Eisenhower playing golf in Baja California, Mexico, 1963. (Courtesy Dwight D. Eisenhower Library)
2 Eisenhower's red, white, and blue golf bag.
3 Former president Lyndon Johnson returned to the classroom on April 27, 1970, to talk with students at Southwest Texas State University, his alma mater.
(Courtesy Lyndon Baines Johnson Library)
4 Jimmy Carter meeting village chiefs in the Gara Rikta District of Ethiopia, August 1997. (Courtesy Carter Center)
5 Former president Richard Nixon visiting the People's Republic of China, 1979. (Courtesy Richard Nixon Library and Birthplace)

BILL CLINTON AND PHILANTHROPY

Since leaving the White House in 2001, President Clinton has focused much of his attention to public service. The William J. Clinton Foundation is focused on finding solutions to climate change, HIV/AIDS in the developing world, childhood obesity, economic opportunity in the United States, and economic development in Africa and Latin America. In addition to his Foundation work, President Clinton joined with former President Bush to help with relief and recovery following the tsunami in the Indian Ocean, and to lead a nationwide fundraising effort in the wake of Hurricane Katrina. He also served as U.N. Special Envoy for Tsunami Recovery from 2005 to 2007.

President Clinton greets Rwandan youth as part of a 2006 7-country visit to view Clinton Foundation initiatives in Africa. (Courtesy of Ralph Alswang/ Clinton Foundation)

Not since the Civil War have so many former presidents lived to witness the administration of a sitting president. This remarkable April 1994 photograph shows President Bill Clinton and First Lady Hillary Clinton, George and Barbara Bush, Ronald and Nancy Reagan, Jimmy and Rosalynn Carter, and Gerald and Betty Ford gathered together on the somber occasion of the funeral of Richard Nixon.

These seasoned men and women know well the central ambiguity of the presidency: that the soaring majesty of the office, its breathtaking power and promise, is leavened with equal measures of challenge and trouble, hard work and sacrifice, dashed hopes and dreams. The presidency, in the end, is truly "a glorious burden." (Courtesy Richard Nixon Library and Birthplace)

FURTHER READING

Blaisdell, Thomas C., Jr., and Peter Salz. *The American Presidency in Political Cartoons, 1779–1976.* Berkeley: University Art Museum, University of California, Berkeley, 1976.

Blumenthal, Sidney. *The Permanent Campaign.* Boston: Beacon Press, 1979.

Brallier, Jess, and Sally Chabert. *Presidential Wit and Wisdom.* New York: Penguin Books, 1996.

Brinkley, Alan, and Davis Dyer, eds. *The Reader's Companion to the American Presidency.* Boston: Houghton Mifflin, 2000.

Clarke, James W. *American Assassins: The Darker Side of Politics.* Princeton, N.J.: Princeton University Press, 1990.

Cunliffe, Marcus. *The Presidency.* Boston: Houghton Mifflin, 1987.

Cunningham, Noble E., Jr. *Popular Images of the Presidency from Washington to Lincoln.* Columbia: University of Missouri Press, 1991.

Diamond, Edwin, and Stephen Bates. *The Spot.* Cambridge, Mass.: MIT Press, 1984.

Dinkin, Robert J. *Campaigning in America: A History of Election Practices.* New York: Greenwood Press, 1989.

Donovan, Robert J. *The Assassins.* New York: Popular Library, 1964.

Durbin, Louise. *Inaugural Cavalcade.* New York: Dodd, Mead, 1971.

Ellis, Richard J., ed. *Founding the American Presidency.* Lanham, Md.: Rowman & Littlefield, 1999.

Fisher, Roger A. *Tippecanoe and Trinkets Too: The Material Culture of American Presidential Campaigns, 1828–1984.* Urbana: University of Illinois Press, 1988.

Goldsmith, William M. *The Growth of Presidential Power: A Documented History.* 3 vols. New York: Chelsea House Publishers, 1974.

Harrell, Carolyn L. *When the Bells Tolled for Lincoln: Southern Reaction to the Assassination.* Macon, Ga.: Mercer University Press, 1997.

Hofstadter, Richard. *The American Political Tradition and the Men Who Made It.* Reprint. New York: Vintage Books, 1989.

Jamieson, Kathleen Hall. *Packaging the Presidency.* New York: Oxford University Press, 1984.

Kelley, Stanley, Jr. *Professional Public Relations and Political Power.* Baltimore: Johns Hopkins University Press, 1956.

OPPOSITE: The White House at night. Photograph by Dane Penland.

Ketcham, Ralph. *Presidents above Party: The First American Presidency, 1789–1829.* Chapel Hill: University of North Carolina Press, 1983.

Klapthor, Margaret B., and Howard A. Morrison. *George Washington: A Figure upon the Stage.* Washington, D.C.: Smithsonian Institution Press, 1982.

Kunhardt, Philip B., Jr., Philip B. Kunhardt III, and Peter W. Kunhardt. *The American President.* New York: Riverhead Books, 1999.

Laird, Pamela Walker. *Advertising Progress: American Business and the Rise of Consumer Marketing.* Baltimore: Johns Hopkins University Press, 1998.

Leuchtenburg, William. *In the Shadow of FDR: From Harry Truman to Ronald Reagan.* Ithaca, N.Y.: Cornell University Press, 1983.

Levy, Leonard, and Louis Fisher. *Encyclopedia of the American Presidency.* New York: Simon and Schuster, 1993.

Lorant, Stefan. *The Glorious Burden: The History of the Presidency and Presidential Elections from George Washington to James Earl Carter, Jr.* Lenox, Mass.: Authors Edition, Incorporated, 1976.

Melder, Keith. *Hail to the Candidate: Presidential Campaigns from Banners to Broadcasts.* Washington, D.C.: Smithsonian Institution Press, 1992.

Pauley, Matthew A. *I Do Solemnly Swear: The President's Constitutional Oath, Its Meaning and Importance in the History of Oaths.* Lanham, Md.: University Press of America, 1999.

Peterson, Merrill D. *Lincoln in American Memory.* New York: Oxford University Press, 1994.

Pious, Richard M. *The American Presidency.* New York: Basic Books, 1979.

Plissner, Martin. *The Control Room: How Television Calls the Shots in Presidential Elections.* New York: Free Press, 1999.

Rossiter, Clinton. *The American Presidency.* Revised edition. New York: Mentor Books, 1960.

Schlesinger, Arthur M., Jr., ed. *Running for President: The Candidates and Their Images.* 2 vols. New York: Simon and Schuster, 1994.

Shogan, Robert. *The Double-Edged Sword: How Character Makes and Ruins Presidents, from Washington to Clinton.* Boulder, Colo.: Westview Press, 1999.

Smith, Richard Norton. *Patriarch: George Washington and the New Nation.* Boston: Houghton Mifflin, 1993.

Starling, Edmund W. *Starling of the White House: The Story of the Man Whose Secret Service Detail Guarded Five Presidents from Woodrow Wilson to Franklin D. Roosevelt.* New York: Simon and Schuster, 1946.

Van Rijn, Guido. *Roosevelt's Blues: African-American Blues and Gospel Songs on FDR.* Jackson: University Press of Mississippi, 1997.

Watson, Mary Ann. *The Expanding Vista: American Television in the Kennedy Years.* Durham, N.C.: Duke University Press, 1994.

Weichmann, Louis J. *A True History of the Assassination of Abraham Lincoln and the Conspiracy of 1865.* New York: Vintage Books, 1977.

Wood, Gordon S. *The Creation of the American Republic, 1776–1787.* New York: W. W. Norton, 1969.

Ivory-handled letter seal used by President James K. Polk.

A PRESIDENTIAL CHRONOLOGY

NO.	NAME	YEARS IN OFFICE	VICE PRESIDENT
1	George Washington (1732–1799)	1789–1797	John Adams
2	John Adams (1735–1826)	1797–1801	Thomas Jefferson
3	Thomas Jefferson (1743–1826)	1801–1809	Aaron Burr George Clinton
4	James Madison (1751–1836)	1809–1817	George Clinton Elbridge Gerry
5	James Monroe (1758–1831)	1817–1825	Daniel D. Tompkins
6	John Quincy Adams (1767–1848)	1825–1829	John C. Calhoun
7	Andrew Jackson (1767–1845)	1829–1837	John C. Calhoun Martin Van Buren
8	Martin Van Buren (1782–1862)	1837–1841	Richard M. Johnson
9	William Henry Harrison (1773–1841)	1841	John Tyler
10	John Tyler (1790–1862)	1841–1845	—
11	James K. Polk (1795–1849)	1845–189	George M. Dalla
12	Zachary Taylor (1784–1850)	1849–1850	Millard Fillmore
13	Millard Fillmore (1800–1874)	1850–1853	—
14	Franklin Pierce (1804–1869)	1853–1857	William R. King
15	James Buchanan (1791–1868)	1857–1861	John C. Breckinridge
16	Abraham Lincoln (1809–1865)	1861–1865	Hannibal Hamlin Andrew Johnson
17	Andrew Johnson (1808–1875)	1865–1869	—
18	Ulysses S. Grant (1822–1885)	1869–1877	Schuyler Colfax Henry Wilson

NO.	NAME	YEARS IN OFFICE	VICE PRESIDENT
19	Rutherford B. Hayes (1822–1893)	1877–1881	William A. Wheeler
20	James A. Garfield (1831–1881)	1881	Chester A. Arthur
21	Chester A. Arthur (1830–1886)	1881–1885	—
22	Grover Cleveland (1837–1908)	1885–1889	Thomas A. Hendricks
23	Benjamin Harrison (1833–1901)	1889–1893	Levi P. Morton
24	Grover Cleveland	1893–1897	Adlai E. Stevenson
25	William McKinley (1843–1901)	1897–1901	Garret A. Hobart Theodore Roosevelt
26	Theodore Roosevelt (1858–1919)	1901–1909	— Charles W. Fairbanks
27	William Howard Taft (1857–1930)	1909–1913	James S. Sherman
28	Woodrow Wilson (1856–1924)	1913–1921	Thomas R. Marshall
29	Warren G. Harding (1865–1923)	1921–1923	Calvin Coolidge
30	Calvin Coolidge (1872–1933)	1923–1929	— Charles G. Dawes
31	Herbert Hoover (1874–1964)	1929–1933	Charles Curtis
32	Franklin D. Roosevelt (1882–1945)	1933–1945	John Nance Garner Henry A. Wallace Harry S. Truman
33	Harry S. Truman (1884–1972)	1945–1953	— Alben W. Barkley
34	Dwight D. Eisenhower (1890–1969)	1953–1961	Richard M. Nixon
35	John F. Kennedy (1917–1963)	1961–1963	Lyndon B. Johnson
36	Lyndon B. Johnson (1908–1973)	1963–1969	— Hubert H. Humphrey
37	Richard M. Nixon (1913–1994)	1969–1974	Spiro T. Agnew Gerald Ford
38	Gerald Ford (1913–2006)	1974–1977	Nelson A. Rockefeller
39	Jimmy Carter (1924–)	1977–1981	Walter F. Mondale
40	Ronald Reagan (1911–2004)	1981–1989	George Bush
41	George Bush (1924–)	1989–1993	J. Danforth Quayle
42	William Jefferson Clinton (1946–)	1993–2001	Albert Gore
43	George W. Bush (1946–)	2001-2009	Richard B. Cheney
44	Barack H. Obama (1961–)	2009–	Joseph R. Biden

ACKNOWLEDGMENTS

One of the pleasures in publishing this volume is having the opportunity to thank the many individuals and organizations that have generously contributed to the success of the exhibition and this companion book. We would like to thank Secretary Lawrence Small and Undersecretary Sheila Burke, American Museum and National Programs, Smithsonian Institution, for their support and encouragement of this endeavor. The authors are forever indebted to the members of the exhibition and publication team that include: Lynn Chase, Patrick Ladden, Julia Forbes, Harold Closter, Joan Mentzer, Selma Thomas, Frances Dispenzirie, Lisa Kathleen Graddy, Jane Fortune, Larry Bird, Kathryn Henderson, William Eastman, Ian Cooke, Shannon Perich, David Miller, Sue Ostroff, Carrie Bruns, Laura Kreiss, Tom Bower, and the project's interns, Brigid Nuta, Nicole Erickson, Chris Bransfield, Chris Bokulich, Trisha Laski, Zachary Bray, Alex Katz, Nina Moellers, Brigid Laurie and Esther Sung. This project would simply never have happened without their insights and untiring support.

The development of the exhibition and book has relied on the support of many within the Smithsonian Institution. At the risk of leaving someone out we would like to recognize Howard Bass, Sue Walther, Judy Gradwohl, Peter Liebhold, Shelly Foote, John Fleckner, Joyce Ramey, Elizabeth Perry, Shelley Goode, Melinda Machado, Susan Strange, Vanessa Broussard-Simmons, Fath Ruffins, Dwight Bowers, Charlie McGovern, Douglas Mudd, Ed Ryan, Sarah Rittgers, Jennifer Strobel, Judy Chelnick, Eric Jentsch, John Hasse, Bob Norton, Tom Tearman, Brian Jensen, Karen Garlick, Debbie Hashim, James Gardner, Nancy McCoy, Amy Bartow-Melia, Omar Wynn, Matt MacArthur, Rex Ellis, Wendy Colbert, Stacey Kluck, Jane Rogers, Stan Nelson, Joan Boudreau, Anne Serio, Helena Wright, Melodie Sweeney, Zugeily Junier, Richard Siday, Beth Richwine, Sunae Park Evans, Karen Harris, Richard Barden, Joan Young, Lynne Gilliland, Kristie Sweet, Carolyn Long, Debora Scriber-Miller, Gina Cordero, Tim Grove, and Andrea Lowther at the National Museum of American History; Mark Pachter, Ellen Miles, Beverly Cox, and Heather Egan from the National Portrait Gallery; James Bruns and Linda Edquist of the National Postal Museum; Alan Needell, Amanda Young, and Brian Nicklas from the National Air and Space Museum; Alan Hart and Lorie Aceto, Office of Imaging, Printing

President Barrack
Obama on his first trip
aboard Air Force One.
(Courtesy the White
House/Pete Souza)

and Photographic Services; Marsha Shaines and Lauryn Grant from the Office
of the General Counsel.

We are most grateful to the individuals and institutions around the country
that have, often on very short notice, taken the time to contribute to this effort.
We would like to thank Betty Monkman and Bill Allman, White House
Curator's Office; Marcia Anderson and Harmony Haskins, White House
Historical Association; Diane Skvarla, Melinda Smith, and Rainey Tisdale,
Senate Curator's Office; Barbara Wolanin, Architect of the Capitol; Deborah
Evans, Sabrina Thomas, and Travis Westly of the Library of Congress; David
Peterson, Sharon Fawcett, and Walter Hill of the National Archives and Records
Administration; Cheryl M. Robledo, National Gallery of Art; Tina Houston
and Philip Scott, Lyndon Baines Johnson Library; Allen Goodrich and James
Hill, John F. Kennedy Library; Leslie M. Rankin-Conger and Josh Tenenbaum,
Ronald Reagan Library; Mary Finch, George Bush Library; Michelle M.
Frauenberger, Mark Hunt, Kathy Anson and Tex Parks, Franklin D. Roosevelt
Library; Jay Snider, Karl Weissenbach, David J. Mengel, and Heather Mason
MacRae, Nixon Presidential Materials, National Archives and Records
Administration; Jay Snider and Gilbert Gonzalez, The Rutherford B. Hayes
Presidential Center; Thomas Price, James K. Polk Ancestral Home; Pauline
Testerman, Harry S. Truman Library; Susan Naulty, Richard Nixon Library and
Birthplace; Kenneth G. Hafeli, Gerald R. Ford Library; David J. Stanhope,
Jimmy Carter Library; Kathleen Struss, Dwight D. Eisenhower Library; Emily R.
Howard, The Carter Center; Catherine Fitts and Franz Jantzen, Supreme Court
of the United States; Grace Cohen Grossman, Skirball Cultural Center; Peter

Harrington, Brown University Library; Susan Newton, Winterthur Museum; John Medlin, University of Washington Libraries; Carolyn Gilman and Duane Sneddeker, Missouri Historical Society; Aaron Sorkin, producer, *The West Wing;* Paul Hemus and Beth Bale of Planet Hollywood; Robert D. Reynolds, Jr., The George Meany Memorial Archives; Sarah H. Van Allen, The Gallup Organization; Lisa Lieb, Bank of America; Leslie O'Flahavan and Marilynne Rudick of e-write; Mark Robinson, National History Day; Jay Wickliff and Linda Gordon Kuzmack of Presidential Classroom; Ann Grogg; Susan Silverstein Scott; JoAnn Bromley, King Visual Technology; Tom Conroy, Movie Still Archives; John Alvitti, The Franklin Institute; Paul Romaine of the Morgan Library; James P. Desler, Celia Hoke and Robert Scher, Office of Secretary of Defense; Major John Beaulieu, Air Force History Office; Lieutenant Colonel Jeff White, U.S. Marine Corps; Captain Nancy Brown, and Paul Gullucci White House Military Office; Marilyn Jacanin and Ellen Lovell of The White House; Master Gunnery Sergeant D. Michael Ressler, United States Marine Band; James Mackin, Michael Sampson, and Robert Lepley, the United States Secret Service; Congressman James E. Rogan; Stefan Dressler; Helen Thomas; Fred and Suzy Maroon; Thomas Rieger; Barbara L. Gregson; Eric Kulberg; Joan M. Mathys; Bonnie Rowan; Margaret K. Tearman; James Basker, Gilder Lehrman Institute of American History; iXL; Michael Smith and his colleagues at Design and Production, Incorporated; Libby O'Connell and the staff of The History Channel; and Patrick Gallagher and his colleagues at Gallagher & Associates.

We are deeply indebted to Richard Norton Smith, Keith Melder, Donald Ritchie, and Alan Lichtman who took the time to read the manuscript, or to offer critical guidance to this endeavor. The exhibition and book have been greatly strengthened by their insights and scholarship.

Special thanks to President Jimmy Carter, President William Clinton, President Gerald Ford, and President George Bush for their gracious participation in this project.

Finally we offer our profound thanks to our colleagues at Smithsonian Institution Press: Peter Cannell, Caroline Newman, Janice Wheeler, Martha Sewall, Duke Johns, Mary DeYoung, Taryn Costanzo, Matt Crosby, Annette Windhorn, and Matt Litts.

Pen used by President Grant to sign the Fifteenth Amendment to the Constitution in 1870: "The right of citizens . . . to vote shall not be denied or abridged by the United States or by any state on account of race, color, or previous condition of servitude."

A GLORIOUS BURDEN

The initial caps used in this book are set in Castellar, a titling face using an engraved white line within its main stroke. It is a style first popularized about 1749 in France—a period when great cultural and political innovations were taking place. The text font is Centaur, designed by the American typographer Bruce Rogers, and considered by some to be one of the most beautiful roman typefaces ever designed.